ADVANCE PRAISE

'Being a sales and marketing professional, this book has kindled my thoughts on how the sales and marketing functions contribute to the financial growth of a business. The action plan provided at the end of the chapters is a good way to navigate the business in the desired path. *Where's the Moolah* is a must-read for business folks.'

Sajeev Rajasekharan
Managing Director, Asia Emerging Markets and India,
Harley-Davidson Motor Company

'Although the book is titled *Where's the Moolah?* it is not a book that covers just money matters. After all, "money", is the output of the business that gets many of the fundamentals right. In that context, this book covers many of the "first principle thinking" for running a business effectively and efficiently as a profitable venture. Topics such as pricing strategy, forest principle and business karma are examples of what I am referring to, which are rarely covered in other books of this genre. I encourage young entrepreneurs and business leaders to read this book and benefit from the wealth of knowledge which is being shared in this book.'

Suresh Sambandam
CEO, Kissflow

'With the book *Where's the Moolah?* Sangeeta has written a very practical guide for business leaders. She asks and helps answer the key questions facing businesses today while weaving in the importance of closely connecting finance with the corporate mission. This book is a great read for entrepreneurs and business chiefs.'

Steve Rosvold
Founder, CFO.University, USA

'Sangeeta Shankaran Sumesh's book on *Where's the Moolah?* is a very comprehensive work which looks at managing any organization competently to achieve its goals. While money may not be the ultimate goal of all organizations, every organization's effectiveness can be measured with this single most important indicator. Sangeeta has dealt with this important indicator of organizational effectiveness using a multidimensional model which deals with people, customers, markets, suppliers, technology, strategy and, most importantly, finance. The book is a great workbook for entrepreneurs and professional managers of all disciplines. It is filled with case studies and illustrative examples.'

Dr T. V. Rao
Former Professor, IIM Ahmedabad; Chairman, TVRLS

'*Where's the Moolah?* is one of the first books to guide entrepreneurs through a full life cycle of establishing a profitable business. If you deeply care about growing your business financially, this book is a "must-read", since each chapter reinforces successful money management. The author has unpacked decades of experience in financial management throughout the book.'

Ram Nagappan
Co-founder, American Tamil Entrepreneurs
Association, USA

'In the current climate of fast-paced, volatile and profit-driven business ecosystems across the world, Sangeeta's book *Where's the Moolah?* captures the fine prints of managing money and bringing to life its productive use.' This book would serve as a quick lesson/refresher on the essentials of modern finance planning and accelerated business growth for both young entrepreneurs and seasoned leaders alike, who can draw on the rich insights and knowledge which the author amassed through her 25-year-journey in the business arena.

The way the book captures the nuances of money management, profitability and economic productivity in a very clear and simple manner is commendable. Sangeeta through her work has nicely showcased the various critical phases in a business, with real-life leaders sharing their thoughts on addressing the same.

RaviChandran Purushothaman
President, Danfoss India

'*Where's the Moolah?* is a very practical guide to not just making money but also doing so effectively, ethically and efficiently. While the end objective is to achieve financial goals, the author makes it clear that for long-term financial high performance, one has to follow a considered path of setting the right systems and processes, employee orientation, customer and supplier focus, leveraging technology and scale, and doing all these with integrity. The book is a valuable asset to business leaders, managers and entrepreneurs across start-ups to mature and large-scale businesses.'

Srividya Gopal
Managing Director, Duff & Phelps, Singapore

'The biggest challenge for the entrepreneurs today is effective financial management. Books which teach the art of finance offer a great way of learning. Ms Sangeeta Sumesh in her book *Where's the Moolah?* has distilled the essence of the matter and explained in clear and simple English, offering a vast array of advice on how entrepreneurs can tilt the odds in their favour.

It is a powerful no-nonsense prescription on how the entrepreneurs should structure their strategies in the current market environment.'

Neethi Mohan
Chairman, Young Entrepreneur School, Tamil Nadu

'Sangeeta's book *Where's the Moolah?* is a must-read for entrepreneurs, start-ups and business leaders.

What I find really valuable in the book is the focus on the principles-based approach combined with the right tools to actually implement. For instance, pricing strategy and business karma are great levers but most often ignored by business leaders. Any serious leader who wants to establish a sound business on solid principles must have this book in his go-to collection of books.'

Jayanthra Jayachandran
Director, Entrepreneurs' Organization, South Asia

WHERE'S THE MOOLAH?

Financial Growth Hacking for Business Profitability

WHERE'S THE MOOLAH?

Financial Growth Hacking for Business Profitability

SANGEETA SHANKARAN SUMESH

$SAGE | Response Business Books

Los Angeles | London | New Delhi
Singapore | Washington DC | Melbourne

First published in 2021 by

SAGE Publications India Pvt Ltd
B1/I-1 Mohan Cooperative Industrial Area
Mathura Road, New Delhi 110 044, India
www.sagepub.in

SAGE Publications Inc
2455 Teller Road
Thousand Oaks, California 91320, USA

SAGE Publications Ltd
1 Oliver's Yard, 55 City Road
London EC1Y 1SP, United Kingdom

SAGE Publications Asia-Pacific Pte Ltd
18 Cross Street #10-10/11/12
China Square Central
Singapore 048423

Published by Vivek Mehra for SAGE Publications India Pvt Ltd. Typeset in 11/14 ITC Stone Serif by Fidus Design Pvt Ltd, Chandigarh.

Library of Congress Cataloging-in-Publication Data Available

ISBN: 978-93-91370-53-4 (PB)

SAGE Team: Neha Pal, Satvinder Kaur and Kanika Mathur

Dedicating this book to
entrepreneurs and intrapreneurs
who want financial growth of
their business

Thank you for choosing a SAGE product!
If you have any comment, observation or feedback,
I would like to personally hear from you.

Please write to me at **contactceo@sagepub.in**

Vivek Mehra, Managing Director and CEO, SAGE India.

Bulk Sales

SAGE India offers special discounts
for purchase of books in bulk.
We also make available special imprints
and excerpts from our books on demand.

For orders and enquiries, write to us at

Marketing Department
SAGE Publications India Pvt Ltd
B1/I-1, Mohan Cooperative Industrial Area
Mathura Road, Post Bag 7
New Delhi 110044, India

E-mail us at **marketing@sagepub.in**

Subscribe to our mailing list
Write to **marketing@sagepub.in**

This book is also available as an e-book.

CONTENTS

FOREWORD

—

In recent times, companies in various stages of evolution, from start-ups to more established ones, have been confronted by adverse business conditions which have called for unconventional solutions. There is a need to set clear goals, practise fiscal discipline and constantly calibrate performance. At the same time, leaders need to guard against fear of failure, remain motivated and continue to believe in themselves and their vision.

This book addresses all these issues, and more. Sangeeta combines her passion for the subject with the experience that she has gained from several years as a finance professional and a business coach. She starts by taking a holistic view of business, then breaks it down into discreet, functional elements, and goes on to examine how each one of them can contribute to the success of the enterprise. The overarching focus is on growing the profitability of the business and ensuring that cash and working capital management are leveraged towards this end.

The book presents innovative ideas on how to stimulate growth. Sangeeta equips the reader with templates around which to structure their action plans in such a way that all functional aspects are covered and structured to work in a collaborative manner towards the common organizational goal.

The book is very timely, given the unprecedented circumstances that businesses across the board find themselves in today. It provokes its readers to think and introspect, emphasizes the need for them to then commit themselves to difficult decisions and highlights the importance of being able to carry their teams along with them on this journey. It is a must-read for business heads and entrepreneurs seeking to maximize the full potential of their ventures.

R. Ramaraj
Co-founder, Sify Technologies Ltd and Angel Investor

PREFACE
—

Businesses seek higher growth, greater profits and better returns. While it may seem alright to want these, what needs to be done by each business to achieve these is the challenge. 'Where is the Moolah (Money)?', one wonders. The need for financial excellence of a business is sought by the board, shareholders, investors and all the stakeholders, and the pressure is felt the most by you—the business owner or the business head.

Irrespective of the size, for a business to peak its financial performance, it is important to understand the financial impact of each aspect of the business. The bases of business decision-making, the business demands that are met (or unmet) and the business actions that are performed (or otherwise) have a direct contribution to the financial health of the business.

As a business head/ owner, have you thought about few aspects as following?

- Does growth in the top line result in equivalent or better growth of the bottom line?
- What will be the financial impact if your biggest customer ceases to be your customer?
- Is it the best time and in the interest of the business to lay off some staff?
- What is your business strategy for forward/backward integration and its associated financial implication?
- How much can your business grow financially by leveraging on technology?
- What is the return on investment (ROI) on the latest technological investment?

There are situations when business decision-makers have either not thought about the flip side or have taken decisions on an emotional basis. And there are also times when decisions are made without thinking about the financial repercussions.

Moreover, many people find managing the financial aspects a huge challenge. They either have a phobia of finance or find finance boring and, as a result, do not bother on the financial aspect. The easy way to overcome this challenge is to look at finance as a game and see what the winning strategies are that can be adopted by the business owner or the business leader so that finance can be made more interesting and fun. This book aims to give you some of those winning strategies which you can customize and modify to suit your business requirements and grow financially.

The objective of writing this book is to nudge you, facilitate newer thought processes and provoke you to think about the various possibilities which will lead your business towards higher financial growth.

Combining the expertise as a senior finance professional with around 25 years of experience along with the skills of a high performance business coach, the objective is to simplify the understanding of the financial impact on the business wheel as well as to empower financial growth of your business.

ACKNOWLEDGEMENTS

I would like to extend my heartfelt thanks to the following senior business industry leaders for taking the time out and sharing their wisdom in their areas of expertise. The book is enriched by their valuable contributions.

- Uma Rao, Human Resources Head, Medium and Heavy Commercial Vehicles, Ashok Leyland
- Chella Pandyan, Chief Marketing Officer and Marketing Director, Kimberly-Clark India
- Parthasarathy V. S., President, Mobility Services Sector, and Executive Board Member, Mahindra Group
- Venkatesh Viswanathan, Chief Financial Officer, Global Outsourcing, RR Donnelley
- Vishesh C. Chandiok, Chief Executive Officer, Grant Thornton Bharat
- Harish Lakshman, Vice Chairman, Rane Group
- Raghavan Neelakantan, President, Lucas Indian Service
- Raghunandana Tangirala, Managing Director, UDS
- C. K. Ranganathan, Chairman, CavinKare
- Shobhana Ravi, Chief IT, Innovation & Learning Officer, TAFE
- Anand Gonibeedu, India Chief Information Officer, Mondelez International

I would also want to place my appreciation to the following entrepreneurs for sharing a leaf from their entrepreneurial journey.

- Nalli Kuppusami Chetty, Managing Partner, Nalli Silks
- Kumaran Mani, CEO, Tenth Planet
- Pradeep P. S., Founder and CEO, Farmers Fresh Zone

- Asvene Sekar, Business Owner, The Earth Lovers
- Siddharth Rajasekar, Founder, Internet Lifestyle Hub
- Jothi Shankar, Owner, GoTek
- Sagar Makwana, Business Head, JyoAsh Engineers
- Dr Srimathy Kesan, Founder and CEO, Space Kidz India
- Dr Bhargavi, Dental Surgeon and Cosmetic Dentist, Sri Sudhantha Dental Clinic
- Rex Aantonny, Founder and CEO, Rex Cyber Solutions
- Shanthini Raja, Founder, Chairperson and CEO, Rsquare
- Prasanna Venkatesh C.B., Direct Selling Agent, iLearning Global
- Balasubramanian P. C., Managing Director, Matrix Business Services

I express my gratitude to my beta readers from CXO Club—Raghavan Neelakantan, Dr Vasudevan S., Chandrashekar Kupperi, Mukund Kasthuri and Vaishali James for their valuable inputs.

I am grateful to my husband, Sumesh; children, Shrey and Svara; and mother, Sukanya,for their support while I was working on the completion of this book.

I am also grateful to the wonderful and efficient team at SAGE, who have done an amazing job.

01

PIVOT ON FINANCE

UNDERSTANDING THE FINANCIAL IMPLICATIONS FOR BUSINESS GROWTH

Growth means different things to different businesses. It could, apart from the top-line and bottom-line growth, also mean becoming debt-free, growth in terms of head-count, increase in the number of new branches, newer territories, entering new markets, increase in the number of new products or services, cash balance, etc.

WHAT DOES GROWTH MEAN TO YOU FOR YOUR BUSINESS?

I would like you to give some food for thought about your business growth:

- What are the parameters that would define the growth of your business?
- What would be the right way to get started with regard to the growth of your organization?
- While there could be many ways for growth for different organizations, what is the best way forward for your business growth?

- And most importantly, what does growth translate into for your business in financial terms?

Once you are clear with the growth that you are seeking, let us now move along to see what you can do to achieve the growth that you want and how to navigate ahead.

But before we proceed any further, there is a basic and important aspect which you should be aware of. You could be deeply passionate about what you do, may be considering value creation, working on developing a breakthrough, wanting to be the market leader, etc. Irrespective of however big or small your business may be, whichever industry your business could be in, however best your product or service may be, I would like you to take a moment and reflect the very core of 'Why does your business exist?'

I have asked this question to many entrepreneurs, and the answer I get varies from the fact that the business solves a customers' problems or caters to the customer needs or it is because of the deep expertise or the wish to serve customers, etc. While that is true, it is also true that the basic reason any business exists is to make money. If this aspect of making money is not important, then one might as well do charity and not call it a business. Hence, it is important for you to understand and acknowledge this basic fact of why your business exists. Of course, beyond money, the purpose, the vision to grow, becoming the market leader, driven to achieve success, serving customers, etc., are bigger reasons, but making money is the basic reason for existence.

If you concur with this aspect of your business making the money, then let us proceed to see how your business can go about successfully making money to its fullest potential. Let us explore and unravel the possibilities that your business has, to maximize its profits.

For your business to achieve high performance and be on the financial growth path, let us start by understanding the following:

1. How to set the financial goals of your business?
2. How the business wheel impacts your financial growth?
3. What is 'return on expense' and how can you use it?
4. What is the art of making your business stay alive and for long?
5. How to maximize the financial performance of your business?
6. How to overcome business challenges?

SETTING FINANCIAL GOALS

Without setting financial goals, the business is like a headless chicken and is all over. It lacks direction and clarity in action. Hence, it is important to have well-defined, holistic financial goals. The culmination of all the business goals would translate into financial terms. Here is a step-by-step guided approach in defining the goals for your business pivoting on the financial aspect.

1. The first step you can take towards your business's financial progress is to set the right financial goals. Your investors and the board could demand growth and pressurize you despite the market situation. So understand from your stakeholders what their expectations are in terms of growth and what you and your team can deliver. Thereafter, arrive at a realistic consensus with your stakeholders on what

you have crafted for the growth of the business. *An important point while doing this is not to get carried away by your 'wish list' and keeping the financial goals real and practical.*

Remember that while you may have your own challenges to achieve the goals, the stakeholders would want their share of return on investment (ROI) because they have invested in the business. There are times when conflicts arise due to this mismatch of expectations and failed or delayed deliveries, which are covered up with reasons/excuses on why the goals were not achieved. Hence, it is advisable to start with clear understanding from both the sides.

If your business does not have stakeholders or investors, and you are the sole owner, then you are answerable to yourself. Just because there is no external person to question the performance of your business, it does not mean that you are not accountable to yourself. If you want an accountability partner, get yourself to work with a business coach who can also act like your sounding board. The coach can also work with you on maximizing your business potential.

2. While you may not be able to control the external market conditions, what is under your control is steering the profits of your business, within the means that are possible for you. Therefore, plan your goals based on what you can control. It is essential for you to have specific financial goals rather than ambiguous financial growth desires.

3. Financial goals can mean increase in turnover, being debt-free, better cash flow, higher profits, increase in market share, higher earnings per share, better ROI,

higher levels of productivity, etc. It could mean any one of these or a mix of them. It depends on what you want to set yourself as a target for your business and achieve it. It is also essential to understand the impact that each of these will have on the overall wellness of the business. Whatever be your financial goals, it should be realistic with a strong intention for you to achieve it. Also know your purpose of setting the particular goal, as it makes it easier to work towards achieving the financial goal.

4. So what is it that you want your business to achieve in financial terms? How would you quantify the growth that you seek? Does an increase in the top line also mean that your business profits are growing? If yes, is the growth rate the same, better or worse? Think on these lines and add on any other specific parameters that are crucial and relevant to your business, for instance, the percentage of the market share you may seek or if the stock price should reach a particular level, etc.

Therefore, what can be the basis of arriving at the financial goals? You can use this as a thumb rule to set your financial goals. To state it in simple terms, remember the name TOM as an acronym. It stands for:

T: Time frame
O: Objectives
M: Measurement

Time frame: What is the time frame you are looking at? Split it into short-term, medium-term and long-term periods of time. Also be clear in your intent with regard to the duration of each of these terms.

Usually, it could be that short term is for about 12 months, medium term is from a year to 3 years and long term could mean over 3 years. It could also be a good idea to state the goals to all the concerned stakeholders and get their buy-in. Review the goals periodically and make necessary changes as the situation warrants.

Objectives: What are the financial objectives you want to achieve? Define these clearly. Top-line growth, increase in margins, free cash flow, better dividends, capex purchase, etc., should be spelt out without ambiguity. While most of these are interlinked, it is better to state these explicitly. Instead of focusing on many, it may be better to start with few focused areas as the business demands. There needs to be transparency and better understanding for working effectively as a team, with the larger purpose of the organization given the top priority.

Measurement: What are the important metrics to measure? Define them. What is the variance with the set budgets? Analyse it. What are the reasons for the same? Scrutinize them. All financial goals need to be measured and quantified. Whatever are the areas of focus for increase or decrease, it would be good to state them as absolute numbers or as specific percentages for better clarity and create the path ahead. Once finalized, communicate and share with the teams, so that everyone can work towards the same goals.

5. Be clear with your financial goals so that you know where and how your business should be headed. Communicate the goals to your teams so that all members have a common objective to work towards.

Watch Out for These Common Mistakes

The common mistakes that businesses commit regarding goal setting are as follows:

- Not setting clear goals and being busy with day-to-day operations.
- Confusing wish lists with reality and therefore not setting the right nor realistic goals.
- Not setting SMART (specific, measurable, achievable, relevant and time-bound) goals.
- Not focusing on setting and achieving goals.
- Not reviewing the progress periodically
- Not breaking the goals into smaller segments and not sharing the goals to the respective teams

Thoughts for Reflection/Action

- State your time frame, objectives and measurement criteria with regard to your financial goals for your business.
- How can you get the buy-in from your stakeholders?
- Share the financial goals with your teams and ensure all of them are working towards these common goals.

THE BUSINESS WHEEL

Once your financial goals are identified, next, let us see how the different functions of your business impact the goals. Before that, let us dissect the business wheel.

For a business to move ahead, think of the business like a vehicle and each of the business functions like wheels of the vehicle which propel it forward. And for this vehicle to move ahead with efficiency and speed, it depends on all the wheels. Even if one of the wheels falters, the vehicle could get stuck and not be able to move ahead.

A business can be successful in the long run when all the wheels of the business work systematically, smoothly and efficiently. Any disruption or dysfunction in any of the wheels impacts the other wheels and has the biggest impact on the core existence of the business, thus affecting profits, liquidity, financial goals, ROI, etc.

The following functions are broadly the common wheels of a business which play a role in the financial performance of the business:

1. *Customer:* A business is meant to cater to the customers. To state the obvious, more customers contribute to the growth in your revenue and drop in the number of customers is highly likely to affect the turnover.

2. *Human resources (HR):* The people or the team a business has is the greatest asset because the people are the ones who can make or break your business. While people are seen as a cost to a business, they are the ones who can drive financial efficiency, processes and eventually profits.

3. *Operations:* Your business revolves around your offering—products or services—which is the essence of your business. This function is the basis of income generation. An impact in any of the verticals that your business is offering can impact the overall financial condition of your business.

4. *Finance:* The finance function of your business also influences the financial position of it. It could be in the form of arriving at the margins, working capital management, fund requirement, etc.

5. *Strategy:* Your business strategy crafts your financial requirements in terms of investments, planning, goals, etc. By having a clear vision on the way forward, the financial performance of your business can be steered ahead.

6. *Information technology (IT):* This is the era of technology, and this needs to be utilized to the maximum. Technology comes with an associated impact on the financial position of your business. Technology-based business decisions need to have the right balance between financial gains and financial risks.

7. *Marketing:* With umpteen options and wide competition, it is essential to market your product or service in order to reach potential customers. This involves a financial spend that should convert to subsequent income generation.

8. *Supplier:* Without having the necessary supplies, your business may not be able to deliver what it is meant to deliver. There is an associated cash outflow with the supplies, which in turn has a bearing on the financial condition of your business.

The onus lies on you as the business owner/head to ensure the competency of the business wheels so that it can aid the financial growth. There is a clear link between the roles of each business wheel on the financial situation of your business. You need to be cognizant of the modalities of each function and have a watchful eye on each of the wheels, at all times, while focusing on the financial wellness of the business.

To illustrate further, here is what happens typically when an organization decides to go on a cost-cutting spree. In order to reduce costs, most businesses tend to cut the headcount, which is a low hanging fruit. Letting go of the staff, not paying bonuses, decreasing or postponing the increments, etc., do not send the right messages to the teams as the employees feel demotivated and insecure. When there is insecurity among your employees, it is highly probable that the best members in the team would tend to leave the organization, resulting in drop in quality and levels of output, impacting the top line. Further, some disgruntled employees who have been asked to leave may also decide to resort to the legal course, which could only increase the costs and not to mention the extra time and effort with the legal cases.

Similarly, cutting the prices with the suppliers drastically, reducing the marketing spend, disapproving investing in technology and holding all the business payments only make it a short-term win for the business, but in the long term it may not help. Because with such actions taken, the employees and the suppliers sense it and get into a panic mode, resulting in compromising the quality, which in turn creates unhappy customers and therefore decreases your turnover. With this approach, there are good chances that the high-performing employees also look for other opportunities and could take away some of your customers along.

Thus, each of the wheels of the business are interlinked and interdependent on each other. The crux of this book is on how you can pivot on each of these business wheels so that your business gains the most, financially.

Remember:
- When the staff feel insecure, they cannot focus on delivering the best quality.
- When the best employees are not paid what they deserve, they leave.

- When extreme cost-cutting measures are done, the employees feel anxious about their future.

- Legal costs do not just drain cash but also drain time and effort, which is not productive. In severe cases it could affect smooth operations.

- When the price negotiations with the suppliers do not create a win-win for both, there could be compromise in the quality. This in turn affects sales as customers are unhappy.

- Without spending on marketing, attracting new customers could be a challenge.

- By not investing in technology, the operational processes are slower.

- The spend needs to be in a right balance. One should not go overboard on either spending or cost-cutting.

So you are probably wondering if costs should not be cut. Costs need to be trimmed because that is what will result in higher profits for your business. Managing your spend is what is under your control. So what can be the best way forward? There is no one way; there are many ways. However, there is no one size that would fit all businesses. You need to know what will work well for your business, as you are the expert in your domain. The rest of the book will help you to analyse function by function and give you suggestions, provide you with ideas and provoke your thoughts in this direction, which will enable you to coach yourself to arrive at the best possible ways your profits can grow.

Watch Out for These Common Mistakes

The common mistakes that businesses commit regarding various business functions are as follows:

- Focusing only on some aspects of the business and not paying attention and importance to other business functions, thus taking a skewed approach.
- Not understanding the impact of the skewed approach as mentioned above.
- For the business to propel ahead, all the wheels of the business need to move at a similar pace. Yet there are times when the entrepreneur does not take action on the wheels that do not move fast enough, which slows the financial growth.
- Not thinking about the long-term growth impact.
- Being penny wise and pound foolish.

Thoughts for Reflection/Action

Some of the questions that you could possibly ask yourself to grow your profits are as follows:

- What are the possible avenues, within the existing parameters, to generate financial efficiencies?
- How are each of the business functions contributing to the financial growth of the business?
- What sort of progress is required by each function to meet the set financial targets?
- What are other ways and means to enhance business income?

- What are the areas your business needs to develop, invest in or spend on?

_____

RETURN ON EXPENSE

For your business to grow financially, you must know how to manage your expenses effectively. Here is the concept of return on expense for you to use before incurring any spend.

You would have heard about ROI. Return on expense is somewhat similar to ROI, with a slight twist. While it may sound contradictory to expect a return on an expenditure, applying this principle could help you gauge what you can expect by planning your spend wisely. In other words, weighing the outcome of any expense or, simply put, what your business will get by incurring the particular expense, is return on expense.

Let me give you an example. The return on expense on let's say marketing expenditure is likely to be higher, as it could result in higher sales than incurring an expenditure on having a posh office space in a prime locality.

Here is an example to measure and quantify your return on expense. The monthly salary of your business development manager is ₹100,000. After including the bonus, gratuity, leave salary, medical insurance, etc., the total cost to the company is ₹1,500,000 for the whole year. This can be measured against the quantum of business the manager has brought in. If the new business obtained is less than the salary, obviously you have not got sufficient returns through this employment. If the quantum of business is higher than the salary, you need to quantify how much new business you are expecting from the person. Is it a minimum of 3 times or 10 times the salary of the person? You need to quantify it and also communicate to the person and ensure the person is working towards the set predefined objectives.

The idea of thinking about return on expense is for you to note how each expense is contributing to the business growth. The outcome could be tangible benefit or sometimes intangible too. Examples of an intangible benefit could be spending on social responsibility or giving charity for a particular cause. It can also be sponsoring an event for your employees as these are to 'feel good' and may not yield any direct benefit to the business. The point is that you need to be aware and make an informed decision about your business expense.

Table 1.1 presents a sample template on return on expense. Fill in this template for your business as it could give you better clarity on your decision-making. You can customize it as per your requirements. You have the liberty to choose all your expenses or just certain expenses for calculating the return on expense. Because expenses such as material cost and salaries may be essential as they are to do with the core of running your business.

Thus, by computing the return on expense, it helps you arrive at the right balance between the expenses and business performance. This reasoning helps in preventing fiascos by randomly cutting costs for the sake of reducing costs. By undertaking this exercise, it would enable you to take a call on whether the expense is actually justified or not for the business.

S. No.	Nature of Expenses	Tangible or Intangible	Measure Impact (Expectation)	Actual Impact on Business	Decisions Taken
1	Marketing expenses	Tangible	X% increase in sales	3 times growth in business compared to the money spent on marketing.	Increase marketing expenses further by Y% to generate more revenue.
2	Connectivity expenses	Tangible	0% increase in sales	Bandwidth and speed of connectivity improved with higher costs. No increase in business but resulted in smoothness of operations.	Due to the current cost-reduction spree, this expense has not contributed to growth. Evaluate alternatives or slightly decrease speed and bandwidth for cost optimization. Can be considered for increase after 3 months.
3	Team lunch allowance	Intangible	0% increase in sales	This amount is being incurred month on month. It has boosted team morale and bonding but no impact on business growth.	Discontinue this allowance. The amount saved under this allowance can be given to high-performing employees by increasing their bonuses.
4	Transportation costs	Intangible	0% increase in sales	This is a pick-and-drop facility provided to employees. While there is no direct benefit for business, the transportation provided motivates the morale of the employees.	Continue with this expense as it also ensures safety of women employees.

Table 1.1. Template for Measuring Return on Expense

Watch Out for These Common Mistakes

The common mistakes that businesses commit regarding their expense management are as follows:

- Taking extreme views on costs and not creating the right balance for business growth.
- Being overly frugal or lavish and not being prudent with their finance matters.
- Not thinking about the long-term financial impact.
- Taking irrational financial decisions.
- Not having a clear plan on managing their expenses.

Thoughts for Reflection/Action

- What kind of return on expenses would you like for the various expenses?
- What are the important parameters for you to measure the return on expense?
- How will you know if you need to measure the return on expense for a particular expenditure or not?

PROFIT AND LOSS: THE ART OF STAYING ALIVE AND FOR LONG

Making Financial Decisions about Expenses with the Bucketing Principle

In order to have a long inning with your business, one of the potential avenues a business owner/head needs to keep in mind are the expenses. While expenses directly eat away the profits, they are inevitable and essential for the smooth running of the organization. Some of the questions that arise as a result are as follows:

- Is the expense essential?
- When is the right time to incur the expense?
- What happens if a particular expense is not incurred?
- What is the advantage of a particular expense?
- How does the expense help in the growth of the business?

I have noticed that many entrepreneurs tend to either go overboard with expenses or adopt a totally stringent attitude towards any sort of business expenditure. Both the extremes are not required. A practical and radical approach to expenses will ease the decision-making.

This section is meant to provoke your thoughts regarding your business expenses and help you achieve the right decision on each spend. For this purpose, I am classifying the expense into different buckets. Think about the bucket each expense would fit in and then make a decision about the way forward for each expense.

Take a moment to pause and reflect on the expense that you are debating on.

The two major buckets are the *non-negotiable bucket* and the *negotiable bucket* with sub-buckets under each. Evaluate each of your expenses into the respective sub-bucket.

Let us first look at non-negotiable buckets.

1. *Uncompromising bucket:* As the name suggests, these are the expenses you cannot compromise on or the ones that you necessarily have to incur, irrespective of any potential gain or loss. These expenses usually represent

your core values which you do not want to compromise on. Some examples of such expenses include payment of salaries, repayment of loan, etc. What are the core values your business cannot do without?

2. *Sentimental bucket:* There could be few expenses you would want to incur for emotional or sentimental reasons. For instance, you may decide to give ex-gratia to a long-standing employee or bear the medical expenses of a certain high-performing employee. Check with yourself, what the emotional quotient is that you are attaching to the expenses under this bucket.

3. *Investment bucket:* As the name suggests, these are monies spent on acquiring investment for your business. While expenses and investments are two different terms, I am combining the two as you can never be 100 per cent sure of what returns an investment will yield. So an expense falling under this bucket, for example, is in the nature of machinery you want to acquire for your business or investment in the stock market. Before deciding, ask yourself, how this investment will help your business to grow.

4. *Return on expense bucket:* This is what we referred to in the previous section. The expenses that will fetch you a return or a benefit will fall under this category. For example, you may want to incur marketing expenses as you feel that it will help you grow your revenue, thereby your turnover. So the question you need to ask yourself is what the benefit of incurring a particular expense is. And the benefit is to be linked to your revenue or profit growth.

5. *Timing bucket:* The bucket helps you evaluate the right timing for the expense. In other words, ask yourself: Does the expense under consideration necessarily have to be paid now? Example of such expenses could

be a statutory obligation, which cannot be negotiated and has to be paid at the right time, within the time frame. Another instance is that there is no point in incurring customer entertainment expenses when you know that the customer's current year budget is exhausted or when the customer is facing financial challenges.

Next let us look at negotiable buckets.

1. *Compromise bucket:* These expenses refer to the kind of expenses that can be compromised on. For instance, a particular travel for a meeting can actually be avoided and instead completed with the help of technology. So checking on whether a particular expense is avoidable is the key here.

2. *Extravagant bucket:* Sometimes an entrepreneur tends to mix luxury with comfort while deciding on incurring an expense. For example, while it may seem tempting to have a plush office, you need to ask yourself if it is really required. Remember that this is subjective because if in the given example the entrepreneur is in the business of interior designing or if they are dealing with high-profile clients, having a plush office is more of a necessity than a luxury. So take your pick wisely.

3. *Cheat bucket:* Two types of expenses fall under this category. One is where you know that your internal controls are weak and thereby you are providing loopholes for thefts and frauds to occur within the organization. The second kind is the kind of expense you will incur for the sake of ticking the box and not arriving at any utility from the expense. Some examples of such expenses are subscriptions and memberships in clubs knowing very well that there

is no use for these. It could also arise from peer pressure or competitor pressure.

4. *Alternative bucket:* Is there a better alternative to the expense? An example for this would be evaluating alternatives for energy costs, which can be, for instance, windmill energy. Similarly, think about whether there is a process in place to obtain comparative quotes for expenses that are being incurred.

5. *Delay bucket:* Can the expense in contention be delayed or postponed to another date? This evaluation gives clarity if the decision is being rushed into or a careful call has been taken. An example of this can be maintenance costs—new equipment might not require maintenance costs while it is just two years' old (subject to the frequency of usage). Similarly, incurring specific connectivity costs even before the commencement of a project does not make financial prudence.

So based on the above points, decide which bucket each expense can be categorized under. Then take a suitable call on when the expense is negotiable and when it isn't a negotiable expense for the business.

Happy bucketing! If you are seeking more inputs on financial management, you can pick a copy of my previous book *What the Finance.*

Watch Out for These Common Mistakes

The common mistakes that businesses commit regarding their cost management are as follows:

- Incurring a spend just because there is a budget.
- Not evaluating the real benefits of a particular spend.

- Not pausing and reflecting how a spend can add value to the business.
- Taking impulsive decisions without thinking about the financial feasibility.
- Too many layers of processes for seeking approvals of a spend.
- Not thinking about the financial impact of a cost.

Thoughts for Reflection/Action

- Set the criteria for expenses that will fall under the negotiable and non-negotiable buckets.
- What other buckets will be required by your business to classify any other expenses?
- How will you control your expenses based on this bucketing principle?

FINANCIAL GROWTH AND FINANCIAL HIGH PERFORMANCE

A common thought process of business owners and business heads on financial high performance is that they deem it to be all-round growth of the business. They want the business to double or triple in a very short span. While it is not impossible, can this pattern be repeated year on year? Financial high performance should be consistent. As referred in the previous section, apart from the top-line and bottom-line growth, financial growth could also refer to the growth of customers, number of branches, newer geographies, growth in the headcount, growth in the net worth, growth between periods, growth in market share, etc., apart from profit growth.

Therefore, you need to be specific on identifying the right areas for financial growth and financial high performance. While the financial growth in any of these areas could result in, say, increase in revenue, it may not always translate to growth in profits. It could also be different in the short-term and long-term period. Therefore, the point is to be clear on the areas you want financial growth and the subsequent impact. It would be best to align it with your overall financial goals, so that you can focus on what is essential.

What Is Financial High Performance?

Financial high performance means achieving superior results by performing at a high standard in financial terms. The superior results referred here are the results that you have set yourself to achieve. The targeted superior results have to be in line with your business potential. So if you think your business can achieve a realistic top-line growth of only 10 per cent in the current scenario, that is the superior result you want to achieve. You work towards achieving the set targeted result by performing at a high standard. Therefore, financial high performance means applying prudence in achieving better financial results as per the financial targets that you have set for your business.

Note that while it may be good to set big target growth numbers, the target you are setting should be possible to achieve (not a wish list) within the set time frame. It should motivate you (and your team) to accomplish them and not intimidate from achieving it.

Further, the areas of financial high performance can keep evolving over time. The business will greatly benefit with small consistent progress in each area as cumulatively it will translate to sizeable financial growth.

On a lighter note, the financial goal set by an entrepreneur was to pay huge taxes. When questioned why this was his goal, he decoded that paying huge tax means that he is making huge profits!! So you can have various parameters for financial growth and financial high performance.

Watch Out for These Common Mistakes

The common mistakes that businesses commit regarding financial high performance are as follows:

- Not setting the right growth areas for business.
- Not taking into account the holistic aspects of the business.
- Missing the big picture and spending too much time on the minute details.
- Not taking stock of periodic progress.
- Not being consistent on high performance.
- Getting distracted on firefighting in the day-to-day issues.

Thoughts for Reflection/Action

- State the areas and the financial growth you seek in your business.

- Differentiate these based on your wish list and the realistic financial growth that you want for your business.
- If required, get a stakeholder or a peer or a coach to challenge you on the set growth.

BUSINESS CHALLENGES

At a time when you thought you are getting a hang of your business and everything seems hunky-dory, you land up with more challenges. The volatility in customers' demand impacts your production quantities. You are uncertain if the long-standing customers would continue their business relation with you. You find the complexities of the regulations and the compliance aspects difficult to comply with. You realize that you do not know many aspects of the business and are unable to get to the root cause of the issues, which makes you feel the ambiguity. You are worried to start anything new or make any changes to the existing business, as you feel it could be risky for the business. To make it worse, there are disruptions happening in your industry and you are concerned if you would be out of business very soon, making you feel burdened and out of control. And if you do not address your business challenges, your business will not be able to seek the financial growth that you want.

VUCA is a term that originated from the US military, standing for volatile, uncertain, complex and ambiguous. This term is now commonly used in business too. Going a step ahead, since there exist risks, plus with so many disruptions happening, it can now be stated that we are living in a VUCARD world (volatile, uncertain, complex, ambiguous, risky and disruptive).

When faced with VUCARD, it is not abnormal for you to feel these.

- Volatility could make you feel Vulnerable.
- Uncertainty could make you feel Uneasy.
- Complexity could make you feel Confused.
- Ambiguity could make you feel Anxious.
- Risk could make you feel Restless.
- Disruption could leave you with a feeling of Despair.

Instead of being bogged down by these feelings and getting overwhelmed, how about thinking about the possibilities and the solutions to overcome these? You may wonder, in the given circumstances how to combat VUCARD? Fight VUCARD with another VUCARD.

The way to manage *volatility* is by having a *vision* for the path ahead and specially to see what sort of *value* you would like your business to provide. When the vision for the value is clear, then it is easier to handle volatility. When all the businesses in the world were affected by the lockdown due to the coronavirus pandemic, there have been few businesses who have continued to perform well if not soar high. A classic example is Zoom, a video platform company based in the USA. Not just the usage but also the share prices soared. While other businesses were trending south, Zoom grew because it brought people together virtually. Therefore, your business must be able to add a lot of value to the customer and solve their problems.

When there is *uncertainty*, you need to ensure you *understand* what is going on by possibly stepping into your customers' shoes. You can also check what is *unique* about your business. Why should your customer come to you and not to your competitor? What is the edge your business has? If you are uncertain about the market requirements, learn to pivot. The example I would share is that of CavinKare, which is also into personal care products. The business realized that the customers' need for hand sanitizers has grown due to the pandemic and therefore pivoted to suit the situation right at the start of the lockdown.

If you are experiencing *complexity* in your business, what you require is *clarity.* How can you *create* the required clarity you want? You can probably consider having a coach, mentor, advisor, consultant, expert, etc., who would be able to help you with the required clarity that you are seeking. Sometimes the Government's rules and regulations, laws etc. may seem too complex to comprehend. However, you can obtain the required clarity by reaching out to an expert who can help you with your requirements.

To handle *ambiguity*, you have to adopt the *agile* culture within your organization, thereby having an *advantage* to think on your feet and make the right decisions for your business. How are you encouraging innovations, allowing the business to learn from mistakes, etc.? The customer service representative of many online portals, even if they do not know an answer, check and update the customer due to their agility. Our country is known for 'jugaad', where we have people like Dr Arunachalam Muruganantham, who has made sanitary napkins affordable in the rural villages of the country. The Bollywood movie *Pad Man* was made on his journey.

Risk and *reward* go hand in hand. What is your strategy to measure and evaluate your risk with your reward? What are the business processes that you are *reinventing* from time to time so that it gives you better returns? A fine example would be when a person wants to consider becoming an entrepreneur. He/she will have the risk of investing in the business with no certain return and also having the responsibility of entrepreneurship. As against these risks, the rewards could be being the boss, better financial rewards in the long term and the pleasure and satisfaction of nurturing their own business.

Lastly, the business *disruption* can be tackled by ensuring that there is a good *design* strategy in place that can be *developed* further along with the changing times. The common example for disruption is Kodak which failed to design and develop new business models. Instead of focusing on the disruptors, how would it be if you focused on your business being the disruptor.

To summarize,

Vucard	Emotion	Tackle	Effect
Volatile	Vulnerable	Vision	Value
Uncertain	Uneasy	Understanding	Unique
Complex	Confused	Clarity	Create
Ambiguous	Anxious	Agility	Advantage
Risky	Restless	Reward	Reinvent
Disruptive	Despair	Design	Develop

Watch Out for These Common Mistakes

The common mistakes that businesses commit regarding their potential business challenges are as follows:

- Not being geared to face unexpected and sudden challenges.
- Having layers of bureaucracy.

- Not adopting an agile mindset.
- Lack of delegation of work and too power-centric.
- No authority nor flexibility for minor business decision-making.
- Not stepping into the shoes of the customer.
- Procrastinating addressing the business challenges.

Thoughts for Reflection/Action

- What is the plan you want to create to handle the VUCARD of your business?
- What are the challenges you foresee that your business is facing?
- How would it be if you were to brainstorm with the seniors in your team in devising the way forward to handle the VUCARD aspects?

02

FINANCIAL GROWTH CREATED BY HUMAN RESOURCES

CORE OF THE HR FUNCTION: HUMANNESS, HAPPINESS AND ENSURING HIGH PERFORMANCE

'People are the foundation of any company's success. People are to be treated like an asset.' These are words from the book *Trillion Dollar Coach* written by Eric Schmidt, Jonathan Rosenberg and Alan Eagle on the late Bill Campbell. Bill was the coach to many of the Silicon Valley big wigs including Steve Jobs, Sundar Pichai and Sheryl Sandberg.

When I visited Glasgow in Scotland, there were huge banners all over that said, 'People make Glasgow'. Isn't that true with organizations as well? People are the ones who make your organization. They are the face of your organization. Therefore, the kind of culture that is being built in an organization is crucial. This internal culture usually flows down from the top. So you as the leader need to lead by example in setting the right culture, attitude and behaviour for the teams to follow suit. Your people can make or break your business. Thus, it makes it important for you to treat your people well, as they are the ones to contribute significantly to the financial growth of your business.

As the business head/owner, you need to explore the following:

- As a leader, what sort of teams are you nurturing?
- How is the bonding within your team developed?
- How can you leverage on the strengths of the team to achieve desired results?
- How are you managing to resolve conflicts within the team?
- How is the trust factor built and developed among the team members?

Having the right people at the right place makes a lot of difference to your business. And shaping and moulding the teams to the business requirement plays a crucial role in the success of the business.

The business function of HR, or the people function, has a huge impact on the finance results. Primarily, the people are the ones who are working and executing the customer requirements, hence contributing to the top line. And the salaries that are paid to the employees impact the bottom line. All the other business functions are driven by your people, who are the core of your business. What are the other valuable contributions by this powerful function on the business? Let us deep dive into these.

Let us start by breaking this function further into four major aspects from a finance perspective and the significance it will have on the business.

1. What can be a good way to derive returns from the HR function?
2. What can be the ways to decrease people-related costs?

Figure 2.1. Profit Hack Wheel of the HR Function

3. How can productivity be improved for better financial performance?
4. What sort of investment on people is needed to maximize their potential?

The answers to the above questions are collated together and are represented as the profit hack wheel of the human resource function in Figure 2.1.

REWARDS AND RECOGNITION

One of the key driving factors is the rewards and recognition (R&R) aspect of the people function. While rewards are for monetary growth, equally important is the recognition part as the human mind craves to be recognized and appreciated and to get a feeling of achievement.

> Compensation is not just about the value of money but has a host of emotions as well. This is applicable across levels—from the juniormost to the seniormost in the organization. Therefore, understanding this human aspect and playing accordingly can help in getting the best from a person.

When a person is not compensated enough, there is ego at play and also the feeling that 'I'm not good enough.' It impacts the status and growth of the person, which in turn could affect the productivity levels or could come in the way of the peak performance of the person.

Does it mean that you have to be very generous with your rewards? No. It has to be linked with performance of the individual. In order to avoid such ambiguity at the time of appraisals and bonuses, it is important to have clearly defined set objectives for each individual, which can be measured, and rewards need to be linked to the same.

What Should be the Basis for the R&R?

If a person has performed well, then they have to be rewarded accordingly. However, there may be times when despite the individual performance, the team's performance or the organization's performance may not have been good. During times like these, fairness in the distribution of rewards must be maintained.

When a person is not recognized or rewarded as per what they deserve, the morale and motivation levels are low. On the other hand, if they are well rewarded, the people are driven to perform well and strive for excellence. So does it mean that your costs are going to increase?

Well, you need to firstly identify the deserving candidates who will be driven by R&R. And by motivating these people, they would be high performers and continue to sustain their performance levels. This translates to a much larger growth for the organization.

When only certain employees are rewarded and others are not paid as well, there is a high probability of few unhappy employees who would tend to compare. You can either ignore such people or, if they are important to you, either make them happy or else have transparency and reveal why certain employees were rewarded well. The choice is yours. Ensure that the comparison between employees does not become a bottleneck for the business.

Therefore, define the criteria for rewards and make it a standard process. This needs to be rolled out for all levels. Clear KRAs (key result areas) and KPIs (key performance indicators) must be defined.

Let me give you an example of how a business can be benefited and a win-win situation can be created for both the employees and the business. Take any high-performing techie in the IT industry. Compare their hourly billing rate to a customer against the hourly salary rate. Notice that what is being billed to the customer is probably 2–4 times more of each person's salary on average. Of course, it has to be more, in order to cover the overheads and other expenses of the business. However, depending on the extra amount that your business gets, you can reward a small part to an employee (say a 10% increase in salary or a one-time bonus), creating a happy employee. To illustrate, say the hourly billing rate to a client is ₹1,500, whereas the salary per hour paid to the employee could be ₹500. You have assigned this employee with the extra business that is obtained and if the deserving employee's salary is increased by 10 per cent, the company stands to gain. The increase can be arrived at after taking into account other aspects such as the teams' productivity, project profitability, company profits etc.

This creates a win-win situation for both your business and the employee. If you do not want to commit to a periodic increase, a good way to reward an employee could also be a one-time bonus or a token appreciation amount. More than the amount itself, it drives the message that the person's work is being valued and it is being appreciated and recognized. This gesture is likely to strengthen the trust, loyalty and bonding of the employee with the organization.

Defining KRA

> In a large business house, a new employee joined as the junior HR resource. He was average in his work but had excellent negotiation skills. Within few months of his joining, he negotiated on the employee insurance cost and brought it down by 20 per cent, which was a significant saving for the business. This cost negotiation was something that was not defined in his KRA. It only mentioned the routine work that he needed to do. At the time of appraisal, he was only measured against the stated KRA and given a nominal increase.
>
> The boss of this junior resource being a shrewd manager included this cost saving into his key achievements for the year in his appraisal and got a special bonus.

Based on the above incident, food for thought is as follows:

- How should you be defining the KRAs in your business?
- How are you measuring the financial impact against the stated KRAs?
- How do you know that the deserving person gets the bonus?

Learning and Development

What an employee also tends to value apart from R&R is learning and development. How is your organization contributing to the growth of the individual? How are you investing in the wellness of the team? Human beings like to do different things and do not like to be bogged down by monotony. Normal gets boring, and the human mind likes to be challenged and intellectually stimulated. Thus, by offering the right sort of training programmes, coaching programmes, and mentorship and leadership development programmes, the individual is not only happy intellectually but also recharged and rejuvenated to perform at higher levels and ready to take up further challenges that could come in the way. This extra leap in performance manifests itself in greater financial rewards for the business.

A word of caution: If you would like the development programmes offered to the teams to go beyond the feel-good factor, you must be able to measure the benefit from such programmes. For instance, how have these programmes contributed to the business objectives apart from the great experience delivered? What were the new skills acquired? What was being implemented into the business for growth? What is the ROI expected? etc.

Team Effectiveness

You may be a leader in your industry, but it is no guarantee for continued success. Your team needs to perform effectively for your business to grow. Some learnings from a friendly, informal handball match between two teams provided some vital lessons that can be applied for success in teams and business.

The captain of Team A was a fitness trainer and was ably assisted by two veteran players and a new player. The players of Team B, including the captain, were average players. At the beginning, most viewers were confident that Team A would win, but Team B won with a score of 15 versus 3.

What Team B did right:

- Quick, alert, efficient and focused on goals
- Teamwork, proactive and excellent coordination
- Gauging weaknesses of opponents and using these to their advantage

What Team A could have done better:

- Lacking leadership, strategy, direction and playing in silos
- Not functioning as a team and not training the new player
- Not learning from mistakes and committing the same mistake each time

Apart from implementing the above learnings for your teams, think about the following:

- What are your teams' actions with regard to the business goals?
- What are your areas of focus?
- How are you promoting team spirit?
- What is your strategy for handling competition?
- How are you leveraging your teams' strengths and minimizing weaknesses?

The financial success of your business depends on the leaders who drive high performance. And the leaders in turn are only as successful as their teams. So, in effect, your business is as effective as your people. Hence, for a business it is essential to have an effective team in place.

Before we get into how a team can be effective, think about the following:

- What is your definition of team effectiveness?
- How will you evaluate the performance of the teams?
- How do you monitor the effectiveness of your teams?
- What are the key parameters for the teams that are important for your business?
- What are the teams' goals? Have you articulated these to your teams?
- What are the challenges currently faced by your teams? How can they be resolved?
- How does the team dynamics in your organization work?
- What are the complementary skills required in the team?
- What are the factors that impact the team effectiveness in your organization?

Get your answers to the above questions by putting in a little extra time and effort. It will provide you with some greater insights into the way your organization functions. I am also sharing with you the outcome of a study undertaken by Google for team effectiveness. Based on the study, the key factors that contributed to team effectiveness were as follows:

- *Psychological safety:* This denotes the safety quotient of the team members. When the culture within the team and the organization nurtures the members to feel safe to voice their opinions, share half-baked ideas openly, be vulnerable, be without the fear of being judged or looked down upon, being open to ask questions, etc., there is psychological safety within the team. The team burnout happens faster when there are no sufficient trust levels between the team members.

- *Team dependability:* When the team can depend on its members to get things done for the teams' goals within the allotted time frame, when everyone understands what needs to be prioritized, when members know each other's responsibilities, etc., team dependability is high.
- *Structure and clarity:* When there is clarity on members' responsibilities, definition of roles, clear structure for teams' decision-making, individual targets to be met, etc., there is structure and clarity that will add on to the teams' effectiveness.
- *Meaning:* By leveraging the strengths of the team members, by giving them the work that they are passionate about, sharing positive feedback, coaching them on their challenges, etc., the members find their work meaningful. And when they feel that the work they are doing is meaningful, they contribute effectively to the team.
- *Impact:* It is human nature to feel good when a person is able to create an impact. Therefore, prioritizing the important and meaningful tasks and helping each member know about their impact towards the teams' goals and thereby the organizational goals will make the team member be more effective.

The above are some pointers which you can use to tweak within your organization to measure your teams' effectiveness. You can modify these to suit your requirements. Rank your organization according to each point and take the required actions to get the best from the team. By doing so, you are enhancing the effectiveness of the team, which will result in better financial performance.

Skewed Performance

It is observed that sometimes in each team, not all members are playing to their full potential. While some of the members are overworked or overburdened, there could be others who could get away doing nothing much or delegate their tasks to others who are working beyond their capacity. This sort of team performance may not be healthy in the long run, as the overworked people will soon face a burnout and the underutilized ones will not be used to their full potential. Think of ways and means to avoid this skewed performance of your team and pave way towards high-performing teams.

High-performing Teams

A business can benefit greatly from having high-performing teams. In fact, every business desires to have such a team.

- How can a business nurture the team to become a high-performing team?
- What does it take to build high-performing teams?
- What are some of the key ingredients of a high-performing team?

Here is a simple framework to transform your team to the next level of performance. This matrix focuses on combining the capabilities and skills of the team members that can result in having a high-performing team. The teams' capabilities when combined with the skills can produce an enormous impact within the team and thereby in the organization at large. How are you leveraging on your teams' strengths? What are the traits of a high-performing team which your team can emulate? Refer to the matrix below to induce high performance into your teams.

Traits of High-performing Teams			
Capability/ Skill	Thought Process	Execution	Management
Leadership	– Purpose driven – Innovative	– Coordination – Monitoring	– Evaluation – Conflict resolution
Communication	– Data interpretation – Success parameters	– Roles and responsibilities – Implementation	– Trust – Appreciation
Growth	– Safe environment – Solutions	– Collaboration – Task completion	– Potential – Specialization

By building high-performance teams, you win as a leader and so also the organization, which can be benefited by financial growth. The team members feel valued and also feel that they have contributed to the organization's growth. The organization stands to gain financially and in the process can reward the teams well.

As a business coach, I have noticed that some business leaders do not like to invest in the growth and development of the team members with the fear that they might move out of the current organization and start a competing business or join a competitor. However, remember that if they continue with your organization, then you are at a loss if they don't speed up and perform well. A business always faces different risks so this is yet another risk of losing a good employee. Therefore, as an entrepreneur/business head, you need to take that risk of moulding, shaping, grooming and investing in the growth of your team members.

Watch Out for These Common Mistakes

The common mistakes that businesses commit regarding R&R and other employee-related issues are as follows:

- Failing to understand that rewards have a deep emotional value.
- Not addressing the elephant in the room such as internal biases and nepotism.
- Not measuring the collective performance of the team or not defining the metrics to measure the teams' performance.
- Not defining clear KRAs and KPIs for the team members.
- Not contributing to the career progression of the employee.
- Not offering sufficient challenges for growth nor offering any learning and development for the employees.
- Not displaying empathy when required.
- Turning a deaf ear to employee grievances.
- Not answering questions on increments, bonus, promotions, etc., thus paving way for unwanted grapevine within the organization.

HR COSTS

HR is a function which can be a great partner in helping achieve your overall business goals. By resorting to effective talent development and talent management, having the right HR policies and procedures in place, defining authority and approval matrix, and providing the relevant training to the teams, HR can drive efficiencies, and this could result in decreasing the HR-related costs, thereby enhancing your business profits. HR must also equip itself with the ability to ramp up and ramp down the headcount as per the business demands.

It would be good to list down all the major costs relating to HR, for instance, recruitment charges, payroll costs, payroll charges, HR software and maintenance charges, talent management costs, bench costs, employee events and engagement costs, and analyse each cost. Review independently with a fresh set of eyes and question the need for each of the line items. Question the status quo. A sample template with few HR costs is given below, which you can customize to suit your business needs.

Nature of Expense	Percentage of Total HR Cost	Justification	Action To Be Taken
HR compliance consultancy cost	5	Required to be complaint with labour laws and other applicable laws	Currently this is being outsourced. If this role is absorbed internally, the costs can be less than halved. Legal opinions alone can be outsourced.
Bench cost	3–7	This cost varies according to the number of people on the bench. This is unavoidable. However, there is scope to reduce it.	This can be reduced 2%–4% by better planning and allocation of resources to projects. This will be implemented from next month.
Recruitment cost	8	As the company is in a growth spree, this cost will be required.	The requirements of the junior positions can be encouraged through internal referral policy where the cost can be reduced.

The HR function should encourage diversity in the form of gender, geography, thinking, creativity and approach for a varied flavour and the best outcomes. This would facilitate varied thought processes, innovation and different ideas, thereby having a healthy mix in creating great outcomes for the business.

There could be other employee-related expenses which are semi-variable in nature such as food expenses, transport for employees, free snacks, gymnasium, team outing and other such perks which could enhance employee morale and motivation. The important aspect is to see how it is getting translated into business growth. Correlate these expenses with the business objectives. Can the business afford it at all times? If not, can it be customized or made flexible and only the most meaningful expenses be retained? Another possible way to work around this is to set an overall limit so that you are able to strike the right balance between employee motivation and expenses. For example, the HR cost per employee should not exceed a certain amount.

Similarly, the biggest costs of HR are the payroll costs. Related to the payroll costs are the recruitment and attrition costs. If the employees are treated well, then both the attrition cost and the replacement recruitment cost can be minimized.

A smart way to reduce payroll costs could be by tweaking the variable and the fixed component of the salaries during times of crisis. By doing so, this could create a relatively satisfied employee, who is also not disgruntled by the reduced earnings. Similarly, by planning the work for the resources and resource allocation, you can reduce the idle time and the bench costs.

Cost Savings

Here is an example of how a corporate manages to save costs, especially in years when there is a mandate for cost reduction, and generate savings.

It takes the total of the HR costs except for salary costs for the previous year. It adds a small percentage to this amount towards inflation, which acts as the base for the current year. If the team has managed a 10 per cent saving in total of the current year costs of these expenses, then the team is rewarded accordingly, thus motivating them to contribute to the profits.

Employee Engagement

Employee engagement activities are also essential. These are all the more essential when the teams are working remotely. Look out for cost-effective ways to engage your employees either for their personal growth or in a way they can grow in their domain or areas where they need to get better such as increased team bonding, soft skills, leadership sessions, useful talks by professional speakers and providing them an external coach for maximizing their potential and growth. These initiatives of employee engagement create a better bonding, and the employee feels motivated to perform better.

Thus, careful and measurable actions can be taken from a cost perspective.

Watch Out for These Common Mistakes

The common mistakes that businesses commit regarding the HR costs are as follows:

- Not planning resource management and the work.
- Lack of proper planning resulting in high idle time/ bench cost of resources, which translates into increased costs.

- Not considering the compliance aspects (like labour law, provident fund [PF], Employees' State Insurance [ESI], etc.) which is likely to result in fines or penalties.
- Not being equipped enough to handle teams working remotely.
- Not investing in fostering team bonding and team spirit.
- Not having sufficient employee engagement activities.

PRODUCTIVITY

The HR function can be the driving force of high performance and resulting efficiencies. Manpower and resource planning come into play for handling productivity. Higher the productivity, higher the probability of financial growth.

If the business is into rendering of services, then time-tracking by the project management office can help in plugging the revenue leakages by ensuring all the work done is being billed completely. This report can also be used to reconcile the headcount between the payroll register and the physical attendance. It also prevents having ghost employees and fraudulent activities in the payroll. It is a good way to curtail payroll fraud. Processes can be automated, which will save time and efficiency too.

By having meaningful employee engagement initiatives, team bonding is strengthened. The HR function can adopt cost-effective ways to keep the motivation and morale of the team members high. Further, importance to employee wellness, well-being, ergonomics, etc., needs to be given because only a happy and healthy employee can give their best to the productivity of the business. Weigh the costs of such elements against the benefits and then decide on the best options. Remember that benefits could also be intangible in nature.

The HR policies should be well drafted and balanced and should specify the approvals required for each, define clear processes to be adhered to as well as convey the organization's values and principles. These policies should be user-friendly and aid employees in driving their productivity.

For your business to measure productivity, it would be good to have a competency assessment framework, which also identifies gaps and fixes it in order to ensure that the best in each is brought out and the potential is maximized.

What are the specific measures, processes and systems that are in place in your business for the people function?

While your business may have metrics to measure the individual performance, what are the defined metrics for the teams' performance? Understand what makes the teams in your organization effective and achieve results that you want. While there are many studies on this, consider it from your organization's perspective and act on what is it that you can do to ensure your teams are effective. Having a good human resource management information system (HRMIS) software in place is a good way to manage your team.

Here are some steps for measuring the team's productivity, performance and contribution to the business:

1. Compute the total salary cost of all the members of the team.

2. In Step 1 above, remember to include extra costs such as leave salary, gratuity, insurance, bonus and other applicable employee costs to arrive at the total employee cost.

3. Apportion the relevant share of the total overheads of your business to each project/team.

4. Total all the amounts mentioned above to arrive at the total cost of the project.
5. Next compute the total revenue generated by the team for the same period.
6. Arrive at the percentage of contribution by dividing the total costs by the total revenue.

Based on the teams' contribution levels, you can rank the performance levels, apportion the bonus amounts to the teams, etc. You can also make decisions if certain departments/verticals/projects are worthwhile to pursue further or not. You can further decide if the particular department/vertical/project's contribution percentage can be enhanced after considering the current industry trends, market requirements, etc.

A parameter which you may wish to consider depending on your team's productivity levels is to check whether each individual's contribution to the team is greater than what the member is consuming. This can be measured with specific metrics such as contribution in terms of billability (or production) and consumption in terms of salary and other related costs. The said percentage can also be compared against other individuals, teams, industry standards, etc.

Team Composition

Yet another way to ensure the team's higher contribution depends on the team composition or the labour mix. The ideal labour mix should be pyramid shaped. The junior members forming the base of the pyramid, people with few years of experience in the middle and the topmost being the leader of the team. This way, the total cost of the team in each project can be kept at a minimum. If the pyramid is any different, resulting in higher costs, ensure you are able to recover the amounts from the customer billing, thereby retaining the required margins.

Conflict Management

In a group of people working together, conflicts are inevitable. However, the manner in which the conflicts are resolved is what matters. If considerable time and energy are spent on conflict management and conflict resolution, the organization's energy may not be used constructively. It usually tends to bring down the productivity levels. Conflicts usually arise due to difference of opinions, poor communication, difference in value systems, competition and personality differences.

As an organization, the earlier you resolve conflicts, the more beneficial it would be, as people would be engaged in more productive work, which will enhance efficiencies. Hence, having a set conflict resolution framework, clearly defined values and the right culture within the business can help nipping the conflicts at the early stage and result in better financial efficiencies.

Outsourcing and Contracting

You could evaluate and explore the options of outsourcing. It is a common business practice, where a part of the work or some aspects of the work are given to either individuals or other companies to perform certain tasks. You need to evaluate if you are better off if a particular process is done in-house versus getting it done outside. Outsourcing has its pros and cons, and advantages can vary based on your requirements.

Contracting of employees means that they are not considered as permanent staff. These people are usually hired for a particular period of time or a particular project, after which their association with your business ends. If required, they can be re-hired at a later date for the same project or another project. These people can be hired from manpower-supplying agencies, recruitment agencies or directly. The contract staff are usually not given benefits that a regular/full-time employee is given (such as provident fund, gratuity and leave salary).

Outsourcing or contracting staff usually happens when:

- You think that there is a lack of in-house specialization or expertise.
- It is cheaper to outsource.
- There is an urgent timeline to be met.
- You do not want to retain the team after completion of a specific task.
- A part of the project is not an area where you want your business to focus upon or it is outside your scope of growth and so on.

Based on your requirements, weigh the alternatives between outsourcing and having the service in-house. Calculate its impact on the bottom line and also take the holistic picture into account, (speed, accuracy, efficiency, etc.) before taking the final decision.

Here are a few perspectives for you, to kindle your thoughts further.

- As a business leader, what is the frequency with which you refer to the HRMIS?
- What are the key insights you have gained from the HRMIS?
- What are the financial parameters you check in it?

- How can you contribute more by studying these numbers and taking necessary steps to better the productivity and efficiencies of the teams?
- How can you arrive at best business decisions by combining the HR data with the related financial implications?

Watch Out for These Common Mistakes

The common mistakes that many businesses commit regarding their productivity parameters are as follows:

- Not measuring the utilization of resources.
- Not thinking of ways and means to improve the utilization levels.
- Not initiating specific steps to fix the productivity issues.
- Not considering the skill, talent and efficiency of resources before allotting them to projects.
- Justifying the idle time (in either getting materials to the shop floor or awaiting the next project) instead of looking at ways to solve these challenges and to utilize the resources in a better manner.
- Not understanding the financial impact of the levels of productivity in the business.

CULTURE AND STRATEGY

The right culture and strategy help in building the business on a solid foundation, thereby contributing to better financial performance of your business. Culture is usually formed and passed on from the time the organization is built. While it is good to retain the core essence and values, there are few aspects that need to change with time. And the changes should be in line with the current times along with the employee needs and the industry trends. These have to be periodically reviewed and necessary corrections have to be implemented because culture impacts the performance as well as productivity of your organization. Think about the following:

- Does your organization's culture enable change, innovation and growth?
- What are the key parameters that are important for the right culture of your business?
- How are you setting the tone of the right culture in the organization?

Remember that the culture of your organization can provide you with an edge over your competitors or otherwise.

Here is an example.

> In a multinational company (MNC), the culture was that one of the top management executives would pull up an employee for the slightest reason of poor performance or delay in completing the work or any such reason and put them down very badly in front of the other employees. The idea was to create an atmosphere of power of the executive and instil fear and discipline in doing so. However, this was not taken well by the employees. The concerned employees would feel ashamed and soon leave the organization. Because of this behaviour from the management, the other employees' morale was also down and the attrition rates were very high compared to the industry standards. Higher officials from the global headquarters questioned the high attrition and organized a survey which revealed the true reason. Immediately, actions were taken to set the right culture within the organization.

Another example of cultural impact on teams is as follows.

Eight high performers of different domains of an organization were brought together to form a team. One of them was the leader. While each of them were exceptional in their domain, as a team, they failed. Why?

The leader did not get fully involved in the project and was being superficial. One of them realized this. He did not want any conflict with the leader and as an unsaid understanding started dominating, leading and instructing the rest of the team. This person had a huge inflated ego and was being very bossy and nitpicking with the other team members.

This led to a lot of differences of opinion, feeling of bitterness, low morale and finally conflict within the team. As a result, the best in each individual of the team was not brought out. All the remaining six members were against the single person. The energies were focused not on being productive but on managing the conflicts. And as a team, the strengths of each individual were not leveraged upon, resulting in poor performance as a team, despite the fact that each person was a high performer.

What added on the above was also because the organization did not have a proper culture to resolve such matters like lack of team cohesiveness and conflicts. People were used to working in silos. Team spirit was lacking. Individual success was put ahead of the team's success. As an organization, there were no initiatives to better the team bonding so that the organization succeeds as a whole.

From an employee engagement perspective, if the team has many millennials, the employee engagement and the culture that is being built in should be to suit the requirements of the millennials. Similarly, while planning the path ahead, the organization should be sensitive to meet the employees' needs and create a sense of camaraderie.

To overcome such issues, it is essential to have a good organization culture, where teams are shaped and moulded to succeed. While there are many tools to measure the performance of each individual, many organizations do not measure the performance of teams. What about your business? What metrics are in place to measure your team's success?

HR Metrics

HR metrics can act as the key to providing valuable insights that can aid in tracking the effectiveness of the human capital as well as the initiatives that are in place. Metrics can be defined for various aspects of the HR function such as recruitment metrics, employee onboarding metrics, cost per employee, revenue per employee, billability per employee, absenteeism and attrition rates.

Analysing the important HR metrics for your organization can reveal the effectiveness and efficiencies of your organization. Based on this, you can take vital actions on aspects such as the following which can contribute to the financial growth:

- How to reduce the time taken to fill in a particular position?
- How to reduce the cost per employee?
- How to maximize the revenue per employee?
- How to enhance the utilization levels?
- How to keep the attrition levels below the industry average?

Escalation matrix, whistle blower policy, employee grievances, prevention of sexual harassment (POSH), etc., must be specified without any ambiguity and must be handled with tact. A constant process of identifying, grooming and developing high-potential candidates to the growth of the organization will go a long way. Steps on the retention of the best talent need to be taken, and possibly new and different ideas for retention can be incorporated. Employee wellness needs to be given importance to, as a happy employee can be more productive and can contribute better to your business growth.

Communicate frequently with your teams and keep them abreast of the wins and the challenges. Generate ideas from the teams. For instance, in an airline, one of the cleaners of the flight brought down the fuel cost significantly by replacing the 'no smoking' sign by changing it to a sticker as against having lights to depict the same. So you never know from where ideas can be generated. Listen patiently to your employees. Exhibit empathy and compassion towards the team when required.

Thus, if the HR function were to consider the employees as their customer and deliver the teams with delightful employee experience in line with the organization's values, the HR function becomes a great value-add partner for the business.

Watch Out for These Common Mistakes

The common mistakes that businesses commit regarding their HR culture and strategy are as follows:

- Not creating a strong organization culture.
- Not doing enough to nurture the culture, talent and bonding between teams.
- Encouraging individuals/teams to work in silos.

- Adopting an unsaid and unwritten way of divide and rule.
- Not creating enough trust and psychological safety among the teams.
- Not hearing the woes or addressing the common issues.
- Not identifying high-potential candidates and investing in their grooming (especially for the fear of the employee moving away to another organization or to a competitor).

Build Your HR Action Plan

People are the most important asset of your organization. Here are some pointers that you can work on to build your action plan for the HR function.

Assess and rank your current level under each line as Low or Average or Good or Great. Arrive at the desired level and the actions that will get you to the desired level. Measure the financial impact of the action on the top line or bottom line or cash flow. State the non-financial impact of the action. If a topic is not applicable for your business, skip that and move on to the next. To prioritize your action plan, segregate between 'must-have' and 'desirable' actions.

Thoughts for Reflection/Action

- What are the various alternate ways to enhance productivity levels and at the same time not go overboard and to create the right balance?
- How can you provide better employee experience?
- What levels and areas of flexibility can be extended to your employees?
- What can be some good ways of retaining the right talent?
- How are you encouraging and motivating your teams?

S. No.	Topic	Current Level	Desired Level	Actions to be Taken	Financial Impact (on Top Line/Bottom Line/Cash Flow, etc.)	Non-financial Impact (on Team Bonding, Morale, Motivation, etc.)
1	Clear KRAs and KPIs for the teams					
2	Well-defined compensation structure					
3	Measure benefits and outcomes from learning and development programmes in relation to the business objectives					
4	State the parameters for team effectiveness for your business					

5	Develop high-performing teams through capabilities and skills to enhance financial efficiencies				
6	Evaluate the need for all the HR costs. Assess ways to reduce the HR costs				
7	Meaningful engagement with teams giving the right sense of direction on the path ahead				

(Continued)

(Continued)

S. No.	Topic	Current Level	Desired Level	Actions to be Taken	Financial Impact (on Top Line/Bottom Line/Cash Flow, etc.)	Non-financial Impact (on Team Bonding, Morale, Motivation, etc.)
8	Transparency and effective communication with teams on business challenges and what they need to achieve					
9	Brainstorm and generate ideas from the team					
10	Instilling conflict-resolution strategies without biases					
11	Seek external help from a coach, mentor or advisor to maximize employee potential					

12	Define productivity measurement metrics			
13	Insights from HR metrics for financial gains			
14	Team composition on projects			
15	Build a strong organization culture.			

LEADERS SPEAK

HR: The Business Partner
Interview of Ms Uma Rao, HR Head, Medium and Heavy Commercial Vehicles, Ashok Leyland

REWARDS AND RECOGNITION

R&R can be interpreted in many different ways by different people. Something tangible is often construed as a reward or a recognition. However, recognition has multiple hues and could vary from a need, to be given all the empowerment and freedom to do one's work without micromanaging, to a promotion, or giving a challenging task to be completed in a short duration, to turning a losing business to a profitable one. A good people manager has to make recognition customized to each member of the team and not keep it common to all the members if the programme has to be successful. The key aspect of recognition is that it must make people feel happy, motivate them and not burden them with an expectation mismatch. Differentiated rewards to the high-potential employees are important to keep the high-performing employees motivated.

Apart from individual recognition, it is important to have a company-wide recognition programme that encourages team efforts, new product launch or other wide impacting initiatives to motivate the employees to achieve big goals. Recognition must be done regularly. Letting the team know about the good work accomplished among peers, colleagues or team members can foster an encouraging atmosphere.

One of the best practices in Ashok Leyland is the Chairman's Award—a very prestigious award. This is awarded to the most deserving teams for breakthrough work. Apart from that, the significant improvements that a team has achieved is showcased to a wider spectrum of employees to motivate them.

Other than the above, any employee has the option to instantly recognize others through very attractive cards which mention 'You made my day'/'You are a rockstar'/'You are a great team player'/'You are appreciated'/'You are a supportive buddy' and the like to recognize team members towards an appreciation for the day-to-day work done.

Thus, it is possible to have cost-effective ways for rewarding and recognizing the employees, and these will have long-term benefits for the organization.

HR STRATEGY

The HR strategy that is being adopted in Ashok Leyland is clear and focused. Two valuable and powerful words are 'happiness' and 'productivity'. Although these words look simple, they are large and in-depth focus areas. It boils down to the fact that the happiness of the employees in the organization leads to productivity, and higher productivity leads to rewards and happiness. This is the foundation of the HR strategy. Hence, having the right skills is crucial for productivity. Equally essential is to become more inclusive and diverse in the workforce with the right people mix. A clear and focused HR strategy is simple to articulate and resonates with the employees as well as the management. By focusing on happiness, productivity enhances, which in turn enhances the financial efficiencies.

KEEPING PACE WITH CHANGING TIMES

To keep pace with the changing times and to combat the challenges of the automotive industry (like the onset of electric vehicles, etc.), the organization is now moving from hiring predominantly mechanical engineers to electrical engineers and chemical engineers, a paradigm shift in approach. Reskilling of the workforce is also the order of the day as this helps in enhanced productivity levels, thus translating to better financial performance of the organization.

SKILL DEVELOPMENT

Skilling the people internally has seen a revolution within the organization, especially with the training and development. Even during pre-COVID times, the organization had proactively veered to online learning, online certifications and online delivery of various knowledge-enhancement programmes. Initially, it was a challenge to convince some stakeholders in bricks-and-mortar company mindset towards this change and also to procure courses online due to their costs, but eventually, it has worked very well, as leaders and team members understood the inevitability of change. Each training programme got momentum internally due to continuous awareness by the HR and sales training teams. A blended model of online and real-time training appears to be effective in our experience.

The stakeholders understood that instead of focusing only on the cost, it is important to invest in courses which are most suitable to meet the department/function goals. Creating internal trainers is also important, as much of the training content was customized to our organization. A goal-focused training calendar should be published. Positioning the training for the right audience and giving it good visibility is a good way to get the people enrol for the course. There is a benefit in coupling the training programme with career progression, which creates a pull for learning. This has resulted in better performance of the organization and contribution to the financial growth.

TEAM EFFICIENCIES

An effective leader must not forget to look at all the small activities that make a difference in contributing to the larger picture. Giving objective targets to the team increases efficiencies and could make it cost-effective too in the process. Deferment of part of the salary, having a variable component in salary, and outplacement of non-performers from the system after ensuring enough chances are given to turn around are some ways that can be effective of cost optimization. During performance discussions, it is essential to keep the relevant data and metrics of performance in hand to enable speaking with facts and figures and make the conversation a cause for positive action. Major efforts are made in Ashok Leyland for manager enablement to lead teams better.

CULTURE

A hardcoded culture of pride and respect for people in the organization is imbibed in Ashok Leyland owing to its long history. Business principles that are being followed are the ones that have evolved over time in keeping with our culture. Sensitivity to people is essential to win the marketplace, and our organization is moving more and more towards compassionate leadership with a sharp focus on productivity and financial results.

03

CUSTOMER-FOCUSED BUSINESS FOR FINANCIAL WINS

CORE OF THE CUSTOMER-CENTRIC FUNCTION: CARE, COMMUNICATION AND CASH

Customer is the centre of any business—big or small, grocery store or a conglomerate. Businesses exist because customers want to transact with them. A business thrives because of its customers. While 'Customer is king' may be considered as an old school of thought, the fact is that a customer is considered as the king because the customer is the one who is generating income for the business. However, the point one must consider is: Are all the customers king for your business? Because it shouldn't be that the customer takes the business for granted.

A good way to gauge it could also be using Pareto's law or the 80:20 principle wisely. Keeping 80 per cent of the customers happy is good but that does not mean the remaining 20 per cent customers should be left unhappy.

For a business to run successfully from a customer perspective, you need to think about the following:

- How do you want to treat your customers?
- What sort of customer experience do you wish to provide?
- How can your customers contribute towards the financial performance of your business?

You need to keep a strong tab on your business and know how customers are treated by your team. Do you know what happens in business in your absence? Let me share my experience here.

> I went shopping to a beautiful family-run store. The shop is managed mostly by the staff and is located within the same compound of their house. I picked some lovely stuff and while I settled my bill I happened to notice that I was slightly overcharged as against the billed amount. Surprised, I queried. The reply I got was that the extra amount charged was towards charity.

First, I was charged without my consent. Next, I was not informed till I asked. And lastly, I do not know if the amount collected from me would indeed reach the needy. There were no sign boards nor any details that were displayed nor the cause for the charity.

How is it in your business? What is happening without your knowledge? You may want to keep a check on the following:

- How do you know your staff is charging your customers right?
- What are the financial controls/software controls in place to prevent fraud?
- What sort of customer experience is being provided?
- What is the business culture environment that is set?
- How is your staff contributing to building your business brand?

You must ensure that your business runs as efficiently in your absence as well.

What sort of processes do you have in place to ensure that your business can prevent revenue leakages, frauds, etc., as they directly impact the bottom line?

Another aspect that organizations must give importance to is that of internal customers. Support functions such as HR, finance, IT and administration must serve the internal customers efficiently so that they can do their best to serve the external customers.

Customers and the sales function of your business go hand in hand. Selling is a function that comes naturally to a few people, and there are many others who detest selling. The sales function is what brings the money for your business through the customer, and hence it is said that if a person can manage to bring in the revenue for the business and keep it going, the person is suitable to build and grow a business.

Figure 3.1. Profit Hack Wheel of the Customer Function

From a financial growth perspective, let us deep dive into each of the following areas to understand how the financial performance can be maximized.

1. What are the ways for your business to increase revenue?
2. How to serve your customers better to enable your top-line growth?

3. What strategies to follow to retain and grow your customers?
4. How to curtail customer-related costs?

The answers to these questions are collated together and are represented as the profit hack wheel of the customer function in Figure 3.1.

REVENUE GENERATION

One of the factors that play an important role in revenue generation is the price point. The price of a product or service is often a determinant for a purchase (unless the item is extremely essential for livelihood or if there is a short supply). Businesses sometimes struggle to arrive at the right pricing strategy or at times even to modify the pricing. And it could be a challenge especially for businesses that are not sure about the industry segment they belong to.

To arrive at the right pricing strategy that your business can adopt, different ways can be explored. You can resort to trial and error on the pricing if you are unsure and check for the sweet spot for both the customer and the business. Some of the different pricing methods that can be tried are listed below. A business can try them individually or even a mix and match to see which is the best one accepted by the market.

For easy recall value, here is an acronym—PRICE—which stands for

P: Perceived value/premium pricing/promotional pricing
R: Range pricing
I: Industry trends
C: Cost plus margin
E: Economic pricing

A quick look into each of the above pricing methods is provided below.

Perceived value can be used when the product or service is looked at by stepping into the shoes of the customer. How is the customer perceiving the value out of what is being offered? By thinking like the customer, one can arrive at the pricing based on perceived value. This has nothing to do with the cost of production or service but purely the value as seen by the customer. It could be driven by the customer's feelings, emotions, privacy or higher value in turn (e.g., higher mileage in the case of a vehicle, better features, etc.). Is your business delivering the perceived value which is greater than the price that is being charged? Is it delivering value for money?

Premium pricing can be resorted to when the brand is well-known and reputed and is considered by the customer as a status symbol. For example, if a customer wants to buy a car, they are willing to pay the premium for the high-end luxury car (subject to their purchasing power). So this price can be based on the brand value. Price is often taken as an indicator of quality, and therefore this plays on the psychology of the customer.

Promotional pricing is when special festive discounts or seasonal discounts are offered (e.g., promotions during winter on air conditioners, refrigerators, etc.) to lure customers.

Range pricing is offering a range on the pricing which can be customized and varied according to each customer. Flexibility of discounts exists in this model. Range pricing can also be offered on a range of products (or services) that are being offered by your business. The kind of pricing offers room for negotiation with the customer. A common example of this model can be seen while procuring fruits and vegetables.

Industry pricing is the most common one, wherein the industry trends are taken as a basis for arriving at the pricing. The price is mostly in line with the competition pricing.

Cost plus margin method is most useful especially for a new industry which is unsure how to price. In such cases, the total cost can be arrived at and then the desired margin is added to it. The total of the two is the selling price.

Economic pricing is useful when the sales volumes are large despite lower margins, thus creating a win-win situation for both the business and the customer.

Apart from the above, the following can also be different ways to arrive at pricing, especially for a service-oriented business.

Time-based: This is the most common way of pricing, which is based on the number of hours spent. The pricing is arrived at by multiplying the hours spent with the hourly rates.

Fixed cost: Irrespective of the number of hours spent, the price is fixed based on the completion of delivery or milestone completion of the service as agreed upon.

Outcome-based: As the name suggests, this is subject to the outcome or the success of the service.

Tiered pricing: Attract customers with very low pricing (or for free) for initial levels and provide very high value to the customer. And as the level progresses, the pricing goes up multiple times. This method of pricing is common for the digital courses and building the customer funnel.

Percentage-based: A certain percentage of the turnover or a pre-agreed basis makes the percentage-based pricing of the services. This can also be like a commission fee or a success fee.

Depending upon the requirement, a *combination* of the various options above is also possible. If applicable, keep an allowance for negotiations by the customer.

Cross-selling of different products or services to existing customers can also prove to be a beneficial way for increasing the top line.

Another method resorted to by many restaurants is by playing on the size of the meal. For example, the pizza or the drink that is being sold in different sizes of small, medium or large has a price difference as compared to the ingredients and efforts involved.

Apart from pricing, different thinking to boost sales also helps. I want to bring to your attention the case of a toothpaste company from the 1950s.

They tried various ways to boost sales in America but nothing seemed to work. Wondering what to do, they ran a contest seeking ideas and had a handsome award announced. The winner came up with the idea 'Make the hole bigger'. Increasing the mouth of the nozzle by 1 millimetre meant the consumption of the toothpaste went up by 40 per cent. This resulted in sales to soar.

A word of caution: – In the above example, the factor of ethics and integrity can be questioned. For all you know, this could have backfired against the toothpaste company as the consumers could have felt cheated. However, business is all about risks. And at the end of the day, the consumer has a choice. So play your cards wisely if you are considering taking this path for your business.

On the lines of the above, here is an experience I had with online shopping.

> I wanted a clothes' case and decided to shop online. I noticed an item that I felt met my needs. However, I observed something on the pricing. The pack of three cost ₹189 (which meant that the cost of one unit is ₹63) and the pack of six cost ₹899 (which translated to approximately ₹75 per unit). Why should the price per unit vary for increased quantity? If at all, it should be the other way, I thought.

My initial thoughts were as follows:

- Is this by mistake?
- Why aren't the economies of scale working?
- What could be driving this pricing?

But soon I realized that there was a possibility that this could be intentional too. Because

- Many people do not check the pricing in detail and fail to do the math.
- The seller could be playing on the psychology of the buyer.
- The seller was tempting the buyer to buy more quantity.

I discussed this case with few peers. While we do not know the truth behind this pricing, most felt that this seller was cheating by pricing this way, while others felt that the principle of caveat emptor (or buyer beware) was applicable.

Hence, while pricing your product you need to plan it in such a way that you do not compromise on your core business values.

Watch Out for These Common Mistakes

The common mistakes that businesses commit while arriving at their pricing are as follows:

- Overpricing or underpricing the products and services or not considering the affordability of the customer segment.
- Not considering the time and effort involved in delivery.
- Missing to include the fixed cost while arriving at the pricing.
- Not including specific taxes or project-specific costs and missing to include these while computing the pricing.
- Not cross-selling to the existing base of customers.

CUSTOMER SERVICE

Apart from pricing, another way to increase revenue would depend on the kind of customer service that is being extended. Small deeds can go a long way in acquiring loyal customers, which will translate into profit growth. Some customers do not change a particular brand once they like it and are accustomed to. This is common among personal care products and in the consumables.

Treating the customer well goes a long way. Take the instance of the Kashmir Arts & Crafts Emporium in Chennai. Everyone who visits the store is served a special Kashmiri tea (called Kahwa) along with almonds, which is relished by the customers. Treating the customers well with warmth and hospitality helps in building a better rapport.

Timely Service

The service rendered should be in a timely manner. Here is an interesting example.

> An absent-minded executive had checked out in the morning from ITC Sonar hotel in Kolkata but had forgotten the luggage behind. He realized it only when he was leaving for the airport straight from the office. He immediately called the hotel and explained the situation. The hotel organized to drop off the luggage just in time at the airport, thus winning his loyalty.

Remember that this is the age of instant gratification. Your customer does not want to wait. They want it right now. So how are you reaching across your products or services? What are the omni channels you have for your business to reach your customers on time?

Delivering Customer Experience

A factor that can differentiate from competition is the kind of customer experience that is provided. When the customer feels good about the product or service, they are keen to return.

> An autorickshaw driver in Chennai by the name of Anna Durai plies his share auto in Chennai's IT Corridor. What is special about an auto driver, one may wonder?! Inside his auto, Anna Durai provides daily newspapers, popular magazines, a mini refrigerator with juices, mini fan, free Wi-Fi, etc. And because of the extra service he renders, he has become extremely popular and most preferred auto to travel in. He is tech-savvy and has even built his website, which has helped his branding as well.

Know the Limits

In the pretext of serving the customer, one must not overdo it.

> A friend had gone shopping at one of the popular clothing joints in a mall. The enthusiastic salesgirl followed my friend, was breathing behind her back and was giving her recommendation on the kind of clothing she should pick up!

Needless to say, my friend was feeling very annoyed and walked out of the store very soon without buying anything.

Similarly, personal greetings to customers especially on birthdays are something that many businesses practice. However, there is an overdose of such automated wishes, and it lacks the personal warmth, which does not mean much to the customers. Some customers think of these mails to be spam. So a question worth pondering is whether your business needs to resort to such practices or not. 'What is the business getting in return?' is something you need to reflect on.

Quality and Consistency

High performance in customer delivery is a must. This means no compromise on the quality and consistency of delivering to the customer.

Take the example of the South Indian food dosa (a sort of a pancake) by Hotel Saravana Bhavan, which has global presence. Wherever and whichever outlet of this hotel I have eaten, the dosa and the accompaniments had consistency in taste. This is possible because of standardizing their processes.

Quoting the example of Nalli Silks, who pride in the quality of their silk saris, once the Managing Partner Dr Nalli told me while interviewing for this book that he noticed that while a customer was billing a particular sari, a minor defect caught his eye. The customer was oblivious to the minor defect. Yet as the brand name and reputation of quality was extremely important, he advised the customer not to pick that particular sari and got it replaced for the customer.

Thus, the way you treat your customer matters a lot in both acquiring new customers and retaining the existing ones. By rendering efficient customer service, your revenue can grow. If you would like to deep dive more into customer service, you can read *Uplifting Service* by The New York Times bestseller Ron Kaufman.

Potential Winning Formula

A winning formula for attracting the customers in the B2C segment (business-to-customer segment) is a mix of combining modern aspects such as design, experience and branding with the traditional aspects of personalization, warmth and relationship. And for attracting B2B (business-to-business) customers, your business needs to have a modern approach of human and digital interaction, as well as adapt and customize to requirements by creating win-win strategies.

Revenue Growth

For your sales to grow, apart from the tangible factors such as quality, features and design, the intangible factors such as customer relationship, trust and brand value play a crucial role in driving sales over a period.

- If both the tangible and intangible factors are low, it results in low volumes of sales.
- If the tangible factors are high and intangible factors are low, it results only in moderate volume of sales.
- If the tangible factors are low and intangible factors are high, it results only in short-term growth but fails in the long term.
- When both the tangible and intangible factors are high, the sales grow in volumes, especially over the long term.

Thus, for revenue growth, focus on both the tangible and intangible factors of your business. Peg your business on the graph presented in Figure 3.2 and work towards enhancing the sales volumes for better revenue growth. Strategize on how to improve the tangible and intangible factors of your business.

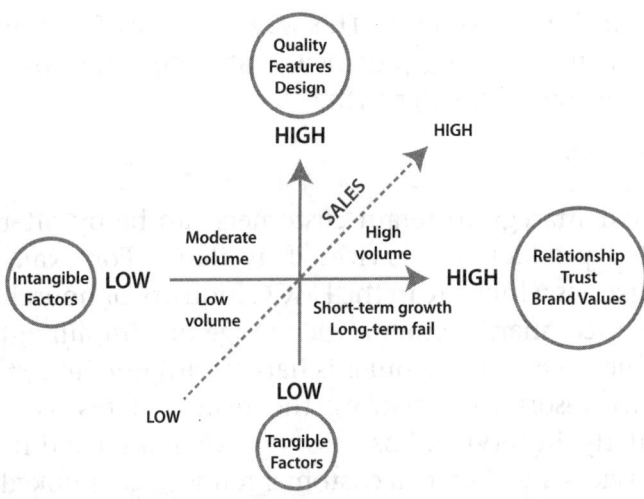

Figure 3.2. Sales Growth versus Tangible and Intangible Factors

Watch Out for These Common Mistakes

The common mistakes that businesses commit while providing customer service are as follows:

- Not creating an emotional connect with the customer.
- Missing to go back to the previous customer again for newer products or services.
- Not providing the best customer experience.
- Focusing on new customers and neglecting the old customers.
- Not building a long-term rapport with the customers.

GROWING CUSTOMER BASE

As important as obtaining new customers is retaining the existing ones. Many businesses focus on acquiring new customers but miss to serve the existing ones. If small efforts are taken to retain the existing clients, long-term relationship can be built. This way, the pool of customers will include existing plus new customers, and you will have steady revenue growth.

Cross-sell

A good strategy to retain customers can be by offering related products or services if available. For example, companies which are in the FMCG industry or household appliances manufacture a wide range of complimentary products. Once a customer is happy with one item, they mostly resort to procuring the related items as well. Similarly, in services business too, when a related range of services are offered, a customer tends to get hooked on to the business.

Understanding the Customer

To retain customers, it is essential to connect with the customers by understanding what the customer feels, address the customer's pain points, what the customer is looking for, etc. A notable example is that of the CHIK shampoo revolution by CavinKare. They introduced the concept of shampoos in sachets so that it could be bought by people of the lower-income strata. Not just that, the users found it extremely convenient, especially while travelling as it did not spill. Thus, by understanding what the customers want and catering to their needs specifically, a business can be successful in growing its revenues.

Tricks That Work

Depending on your business challenges, discover tricks that will work for you. For example,

> A small shop in Chennai dealing in cosmetic jewellery for women had the constant issue of their customers negotiating and seeking discounts on purchase. To overcome this, the shop owner put up a poster above the billing counter which read 'Customer is the king and kings do not bargain nor ask for discounts!' He saw an improvement in the turnover after putting this up!

So think creatively and build systems that will work for your business.

Measure the Customer Experience

A very good metric to measure your customer experience is the Net Promoter Score (NPS). It predicts growth and is a proven method that businesses adopt. The scorecard asks the customer 'How likely the customer will recommend the product or service to someone else on a scale of 10?' (The loyal enthusiasts will opt for a score of 9 or 10, and the unhappy customers will provide a score of 6 or lesser). This can be a good way to benchmark delivering the customer experience.

Although periodic customer satisfaction surveys are being undertaken by many organizations, it is essential to read and interpret the survey results. It is also important to talk to the unhappy customers and figure out how to serve them better. An unhappy customer will not only succumb to competitors but also bad-mouth in the market (and through social media), tarnishing the brand image.

Engaging with the Customer

While many businesses go out of their way to engage, serve and retain their customers, there are few businesses that do not necessarily do that. It could be because they expect the customers to approach them, or because they may be the market leaders or simply because they are using the blue ocean strategy without having competitors or offering something totally unique that the customers flock to them. This approach towards the customer may need extra caution. Read the story below on how it backfired for a business entity.

> Sandeep was running a reputed digital marketing company, which was fast growing. The company was considered a market leader in the particular domain in the city. Well-established business houses which were keen on digital marketing used to approach Sandeep's company for their services. All new enquiries and potential clients were handled by his business development manager, Ganesh.

As the business was well-known in their industry, many potential customers used to avail their services despite the fact that they charged a premium. Once based on a referral from another client, Ganesh had a preliminary round of discussion with a group of entrepreneurs, for their association. At the start, Ganesh acted pricey and had allotted time for this initial discussion only after two requests. The group of entrepreneurs wanted to engage with this company not only for this association but also for each individual business of theirs and were seriously considering the appointment of this company. In fact, one of the businessmen paid up the advance as well going by their reputation.

Despite paying the advance, there was a huge delay in starting the business. When Ganesh was asked about this delay, he threw a fit and answered rudely, stating that it would take time as they were busy with other bigger projects. The attitude and tone of the voice of Ganesh were impolite and arrogant, and no proper justification of the behaviour was given. In fact, he told the businessman not to bother him over a weekend when he called to check on the progress on a Saturday.

His attitude cheesed off the businessman who immediately withdrew his business from the company. Not only that, the other potential business from the association as well as the others from the group chose not to work with the company. As a result, the business lost four huge orders which were almost confirmed as well as a loss of reputation in the market.

Watch out for such cases and equip your team well to handle such cases.

Not just obtaining clients but the after-sales service rendered is equally important, if not more important.

This is what helps build and cement long-term relationships with the customers. If any of your customers are in genuine trouble, extend discounts or credit facilities to them during their time of need. Provide options to your customers of settling your dues in tranches if they are in financial trouble. These small acts will go a long way in building trust, rapport and loyalty with your customer. Delivering consumer delight provides your business with an extra edge over competition.

Role of CRM

Your business should also capitalize on having a good customer relationship management (CRM). It will enable you to consolidate all the essential information of your customers, facilitate better and regular communication with your customer, improve customer service, enable automation, provide efficiency and improve analytical data of your customers.

When customers and potential customers are not treated in a right way, the inevitable happens. All customers need not be treated like a king, but a respectful customer treatment will go a long way for the business and ensure a steady source of revenue.

Expanding Customer Base

By expanding the markets you work on, your customer base increases. Expansion can be in the form of providing complementary services, including related products, newer geographies, offering a bundle of your products and services, setting up franchisees, providing incentives to your distributors or sales partners, encouraging referrals, walk-ins, etc. Sometimes providing small freebies or special discounts can also result in getting large customers. When the customer base expands, the revenue grows.

If finance is a constraint for expansion, you could also consider taking a loan or reaching out to potential investors. Alternatively, if you have sufficient funds, invest in the growth of the business. In either case, do a complete market study and work out the projected growth before taking the expansion plunge.

Watch Out for These Common Mistakes

The common mistakes that businesses commit while retaining their existing customers are as follows:

- Neglecting the older customers in the process of acquiring new customers.
- Failing to deliver a wow experience for the customer, thus making the customer shift loyalty brand.
- Not being in touch with the customer as out of sight is out of mind.
- Missing to update the customer with the latest products and offerings.
- Not taking measures to do what it takes to lure the existing customers.

CUSTOMER-RELATED COSTS

Customer related costs can be in the form of customer acquisition costs, special discounts, legal costs, rework costs, resolving customer complaints, lead generation costs, collection costs, etc. Have an eye on the customer-related costs. Because one can easily overlook these costs while focusing on the top line, and these costs could eat into your profits.

Businesses sometimes tend to overspend in some of the areas such as lead generation and customer acquisition, hoping the amount spent will come back manifold. While it could happen, there is no guarantee that it would happen. Hence, careful analysis needs to be done and prudent decisions need to be taken on such expenses.

A good way to evaluate such expenses would be to understand the past trends, compare the industry norms as well as understand the market potential before blindly spending the amount.

To be successful in converting leads and retaining them as customers thereafter, a business can follow the 3W model.

WOO: Woo the customer with irresistible offers.

WOW: Wow the customer with right product/service and experience.

WIN: Win over the customer for long term.

Here is an example.

According to Shanthini Raja, Founder and CEO of Rsquare in Bahrain, dealing in selling cheque-printing software, they found it a challenge to sell the software to more customers. It was due to the fact that the printer required specific configuration for each of the customer's printer. It was time-consuming and as a result, they were unable to convert the potential leads as customers because the leads did not want to configure the printer for the sake of the software. This prompted Rsquare to give free preconfigured printers along with the cheque-printing software, which not only increased the sales by 9 times compared to the previous year but also the profits increased by 40 per cent. This move also reduced the resource time to implement the software.

Collections

By not collecting dues from customers on time, the working capital of the business is impacted. Proper systems are needed to be in place for regular follow-up of monies due. Legal disputes with customers can take forever to get resolved. Your business needs to evaluate if it is worth the time, effort and money before taking the legal course of action.

Understanding Financial Implications

As a thumb rule, before incurring any customer-related expenses, your business should evaluate the outcome and the implications of incurring the cost versus not incurring the particular amount, rather than taking a blind decision. This will give better clarity on taking the right financial decision, after considering the business implications.

Provide Choices for Customers

Customers like to have choices. Be it in the size, service levels, fragrances, features, flavours, etc., a customer always wants extra something to choose from. Be it soaps or shampoos to high-end versions of automobiles or economy class versus business class versus first class in a flight, a customer wants choices and options. While these choices, add-ons and extra features may cost your business an additional amount, your business must be capable of making up for it along with a good margin while selling to your customer.

Remember that *a happy customer is the best advertisement for your business to grow.* Your customer becomes your brand ambassador and attracts new customers for your business. It is worthwhile if you can go the extra mile with your customer service and make them feel exceptionally good with your product or service.

Creating the Internal Legacy

Thus, as a business unit, clear customer strategies, policies and manuals must be well crafted, acting as a guide within the business. Documenting what works well with major customers can come in handy in understanding customers' needs and preferences. Building a strong rapport and by being in constant communication with the customer can yield large and beneficial results to the business. This also needs to be done as a team and not being led or driven by a single person so that the in-house knowledge of customers can be a good data bank for further business growth and necessary actions to be taken. This does not cost your business but will be a healthy practice to adopt for the long-term growth of customer base.

Watch Out for These Common Mistakes

The common mistakes that businesses commit, neglecting the customer-related costs, are as follows:

- Not thinking the implications on the bottom line due to these costs.

S. No.	Topic	Current Level	Proposed Level	Actions to be Taken	Financial Impact (on Top Line/ Bottom Line/ Cash Flow)	Non-financial Impact (on Customer Rapport, Bonding, Trust, etc.)
1	Devising (or revisiting) the right pricing strategy					
2	Increasing service levels for customers					
3	Customer experience that is being delivered					
4	Quality and consistency of service					
5	Improvisation of the tangible factors of sales growth					
6	Improvisation of the intangible factors of sales growth					
7	Different ways to cross-sell					
8	Offering customer delight					

(Continued)

(Continued)

S. No.	Topic	Current Level	Proposed Level	Actions to be Taken	Financial Impact (on Top Line/ Bottom Line/ Cash Flow)	Non-financial Impact (on Customer Rapport, Bonding, Trust, etc.)
9	Ways to improve NPS					
10	CRM effectiveness					
11	Ways to expand customer base					
12	Reduction of customer-related costs					
13	Customer collection process					
14	Steps to strengthen customer relationships					
15	System to create internal legacy					

- Missing to understand the impact on working capital and cash flow.
- Not standardizing the internal processes for customer delivery.
- Missing the consistency in the output.
- Not providing a variety for the customer to choose from.

Build Your Customer Action Plan

Customers are the pillars of your business. Your customers' wellness is important, as they are the ones fuelling your growth. Use these parameters below to build your action plan for your customer function.

Rank your current level under each line as Low or Average or Good or Great. Arrive at the desired level and the actions that will get you to the desired level. Measure the financial impact of the action on the top line or bottom line or cash flow. State the non-financial impact of the action. If a topic is not applicable for your business, skip that and move on to the next. To prioritize your action plan, segregate between 'must-have' and 'desirable' actions.

Thoughts for Reflection/Action

- What can be done to improve the service levels for your customer?
- How can you enhance your customers' experience?
- What can be done to go the extra mile for the customer to build a long-lasting relationship?
- Study your customer behaviour. Based on the outcome, what changes should your business make to grow your profits?

- List the customer learnings from the past and the actions that need to be taken.

LEADERS SPEAK

Smart Collaboration with Customers
Interview of Mr Vishesh C. Chandiok, Chief Executive Officer, Grant Thornton Bharat

CUSTOMERS FOR DIFFERENT BUSINESS VERTICALS

We at Grant Thornton approach it as building customers for the whole firm and not just for any specific vertical. Usually our work starts with a one-off experience which acts as a great opportunity for the customer to experience our services and for us to experience the customer. Ensuring that the first experience is great, so that the customer wants that experience repeated, is the best way to grow a business. In our case, we try to ensure that experience demonstrates our differentiators and use that as a basis to see if there is a good fit for us to build a mutually beneficial long-term relationship. It is equally important for a business to assess if the customer is a good fit too, in terms of culture and mutual respect. It is not about adding customers just because an opportunity arose, but the ability to add value to the customer is the key. This strategy has worked well for us for our customer growth.

LIVING THE BRAND PROMISE FOR CUSTOMERS

Consistency of experience is why customers are willing to pay a premium, despite having umpteen options. A customer chooses a brand that appeals to them. Having the necessary clarity on what your brand is promising and owning that territory are important ingredients that help acquire customers. For instance, for Grant Thornton it has been 'Indian companies with global presence'. This doesn't mean that we are refusing MNCs or global companies. It only means that we are focusing on Indian companies that are seeking to adopt to global standards or making global acquisition or thinking global. A brand can be built with a niche and then build several niches over time. Thus, creating the niche helps in premium pricing.

ALTERNATIVE TO CROSS-SELLING

At Grant Thornton, we believe that customers do not like cross-selling and therefore we avoid it. Instead, we prefer 'smart collaboration', where we bring in different expertise as part of each engagement. Today, one can't deliver most compliance, consulting or transactions engagements without bringing in tax expertise, sector knowledge, IT risk or IT advisory skills to the table. Leveraging all the skills that exist within your business, sharing insights with clients and thereby adding value to help the client grow are our ways of cross-selling. A business needs to think from the customers' perspective, which is a much simpler way of finding continuing ways of adding value to clients. By adding value, customer expansion is possible, which leads to revenue growth.

CUSTOMER RETENTION STRATEGY

Customer retention strategy is all about 'non-engagement-related conversations'. This can be in person, virtual or on email/texts. Do we take out time to meet our clients only when we are doing a job for them or even outside that? Are we able to understand what is on top of mind for the customer and what are their main short- and medium-term goals? What are the challenges keeping them up at night? Working around touch points such as these as well as ongoing conversations with customers and understanding their requirements should be the focus areas to retain customers.

PRICING

Pricing is an art not a science as much as us accountants may like to believe otherwise. Normally, rates are established based on a multiple of three–five times salary costs so that these cover the overheads as well as generate profits. However, rate-based budgets only give an estimate, and pricing can be discounted or at a premium based on many factors such as risk, strategic importance and stage of development of the said practice. Pricing is crucial in ensuring that it enables profits for the business. The pricing for a product could vary at the time of the launch to when it is an established offering.

PEOPLE FIRST

Mr Vineet Nayyar's adage 'Employees first, customers second' is something which was initially challenged but now it is appreciated, particularly given the current health crisis which became both a financial and a humanitarian crisis. Of course, customers are important because there is no business without them! However, if leaders are able to take care of their people, then the people take care of their customers. Safety and well-being of the people are of prime importance. In our organization, we assured our people that there would be no salary cuts or job cuts at the height of uncertainty of the pandemic. The same would not apply for say an airline or a hotel, which may not have this ability given the more direct impact, but again how they deal with transparent communication, helping find alternate jobs, giving sight of rehiring preference for old employees, etc., are ways to build an employer brand of putting people first. When employees are well cared for, they serve the customer better, which results in better financial performance.

SCOUTING FOR NEW CUSTOMERS

Word of mouth or referrals are the best source to get new customers, particularly in service businesses like ours. We do very little marketing and almost no advertising because of regulatory restrictions and the nature of our work. Most clients are referred by other satisfied clients. We ask our clients if they would recommend us as a key feedback and use it as a KPI (NPS). Some of us are getting better (less shy) at requesting customers to make such introductions!

CUSTOMER-RELATED COSTS

There isn't a 'silver bullet' to reduce customer-related costs. But by spending a lot of time in understanding the needs and preferences of each client before each engagement, and being clear about what good looks like to the client, makes a lot of difference. That way, the expectation gaps can be minimized and thereby costs can be minimal. Customizing the product or service for the customer bridges the expectation gap. For example, the packaging of an Apple product is done in a particular way so that the customer feels like they are receiving a gift each time, thereby delivering their brand promise.

CUSTOMER DUES

Customer-level credit limit with appropriate follow-up mechanism and proper documentation in the case of taking the legal route are some good practices that can be followed regarding collecting the dues from customers. Very few people discuss invoicing and payment schedules when entering a relationship and focus more on pricing and discounts.

For the micro, small and medium enterprise (MSME) segment, eventually if a customer doesn't pay within a reasonable time, other than in exceptional circumstances where they have a short-term cash flow challenge, it's better to stop serving them than serve and not be paid. Normally, the best practice is also a written acknowledgement of satisfactory delivery of goods and services, and the expected payment schedules, which can then be used to recover the money through legal routes if the situation persists.

FUTURE GROWTH

Businesses don't get into trouble during a recession; they get into trouble coming out of a recession. While most businesses have taken steps to adjust their costs in the short term, they need to reverse any personnel cuts now, as the lockdown-imposed slowdown is over. For the long term, they ought to focus on both new investments and an inorganic growth plan versus play it safe. Businesses could get into trouble 12–18 months after a slowdown, and these businesses tend to be those who are left behind by competitors who choose to invest during a recession.

04

DEVISING A FINANCIALLY SOUND STRATEGY

CORE OF THE STRATEGY FUNCTION: STRUCTURE, SYNERGY AND SOLUTION

> The ambition of the owner of a large business house was only to make more money. He did not have any defined views or thoughts about the business nor its growth. He was busy firefighting the day-to-day business issues. Neither he nor the team had a vision, and they did not think about the future. This resulted in the business being stagnant and over time slow dip in the growth of the business. It was much later that he realized the need and importance of having a strategy in place for business growth.

A strategy is the plan of action to achieve the results that you want. Hence, for an organization, it is essential to have a clear strategy defining the path ahead. All the major aspects of the business such as strategy for investment, risk mitigation strategy, customer acquisition strategy, transformation strategy, competition strategy, growth strategy, innovation strategy, blue ocean strategy and applicable strategies have to be clearly defined. This will act as the base, which can later be customized as per the situation the business is facing.

As the business owner/head, you need to understand the following:

- What makes having a strategy important for your organization?
- How can having a clearly defined strategy help your business in the long term?
- How does the future of your business appear to you?

> Your business starts with a strategy and ends with financial gains. To expand on it, a strategy defines acquiring of customers through the business operations supported by HR, with the help of marketing, using IT and transacting with suppliers for financial gains.

The strategy can also be designed by the functions of the business, all of which should be in line with the big picture of the business. For example, the operational strategy of each business function or the business unit should be aligned with the overall corporate strategy.

When you are strategizing to develop or improvise a process, product or service design, a good management method to follow would be the PDCA cycle, where

- P stands for plan, denoting identifying the problem and finding process inefficiencies and developing potential solutions.
- D for do, meaning implementing the solution.
- C for check, if the new process is delivering better efficiencies.

- A for act, referring to implementing it for the entire organization.

A great way to build your strategy would be to brainstorm with your senior team and then percolate it to the rest of the organization.

You can also prepare a business model canvas (popularly known as BMC) for your business, as it would help you in defining clear strategies for the main areas of the business.

If the strategy is an acronym, it should have the following as parameters:

- S: Shareholders' value to be maximized
- T: Tools and technology for growth
- R: ROI to be maximum
- A: Action plan for the path ahead
- T: Team for implementation
- E: Evaluation of performance and measurement yardsticks
- G: Goals to be reviewed
- Y: Year-on-year plan for success

So what impact does a strategy have from the financial perspective?

A strategy is what will lead to the financial growth of a business. Without having proper plans in place, the business is probably geared for short-term but not for long-term growth. To broadly envision strategy from the financial angle, few aspects that can be considered are as follows:

1. What is the financial investment that is required for the business?
2. What is the basis of financial growth strategy?
3. What sort of financial planning is needed?
4. What are the financial risks involved?

Figure 4.1. Profit Hack Wheel of the Strategy Function

The answers to the above questions are collated together and are represented as the profit hack wheel of the strategy function in Figure 4.1.

FUTURE OF BUSINESS

A strategy plays a vital role in the long-term growth of the business. It can act as the blueprint to propel the business ahead. Therefore, it is essential to plan the different aspects of the business by planning for the future needs for the growth that is required. If a business is thinking of scaling up, without a proper strategy in place, it may not be able to get to the desired results.

By synergizing the strategy with innovation, organizations are better geared to generate profits, thus leading to value creation for the shareholders. Further, by having a clear strategy of the business requirements, better visibility emerges in the actions to be taken, better decision-making as well as the desired results.

What does the future of your business seem to you and the management team? What actions are required to navigate the business in the chosen path?

Organizations such as Apple, Google and Disney are constant innovators. They spend huge amounts on innovation as well as research and development. By investing in the future of the business through a innovation strategy as well as research and development, these companies are constantly evolving. These huge organizations being cash-rich may have the affordability. What about smaller businesses that do not have much money to invest in their future growth, you may wonder?

Let me give you the example of a pushcart vegetable vendor, who was desirous of growing his business. He did not have enough money at his disposal. But he wanted to grow and wanted to set up his own vegetable mart. Considering his financial strata, he could not get any loans nor any investors. What strategy did he adopt to grow to the next level?

With the high-rise residential apartments, he realized that many households did not know he had arrived for selling vegetables. They also did not know what vegetables he was selling and at what price. So he resorted to a simple jugaad to overcome this issue which was a deterrent to his growth. On his mobile phone, he would record a voice message with the vegetables available for that day and the pricing for the day. He kept a loudspeaker by the side of his mobile which would reach the high-storeyed apartment, thus attracting his customers to buy from him. This simple change in his strategy not only enabled him to grow his sales but also gave him the flexibility to attend to his customer while the mobile and the loudspeaker simultaneously did their job.

So for designing your strategy, cash need not be a great constraint. However, it cannot be denied that cash is required. Also, even if a business is cash-rich, how much cash can be added on towards innovation, research and growth? To state simply, it will be based on the availability of cash towards this purpose. Should it be the entire cash that is available or a part of it? The decision can be arrived at based on the financial progress and by setting a limit on the amount to be invested towards this purpose. A suitable amount can also be set aside for scaling, training and investing in the right resources. If your business is not future-ready, it is probable that it may not survive or thrive financially in the long term.

Your business has to plan ahead, understand the industry trends, interpret the analytics and project the futuristic projections. Further, if you are in the B2B business, you could check on the demands of your customers' customers, which could be a good indicator for your business. And to plan better, check the same for your suppliers' suppliers, so that you do not run short of raw materials for your business.

There are times when you need to create the future of your business from a long-term perspective, which you need to strategize. For instance, your sales strategy should include some of the following:

- What is different about your business?
- Why should your customer buy from you and not your competition?
- What is your unique selling point (USP)?

- What are the added advantages your business offers to the customers?
- What are the different strategies/new strategies that are being adopted to increase sales?

I have noticed that while many entrepreneurs know the answers to the above questions, they fail to highlight the uniqueness and therefore it does not translate into desired sales. It is important to define your clear sales strategy and communicate it to your teams too so that everyone speaks the same business language to the customers.

To be up in the game and future-ready, Murugappa Group, one of India's leading business conglomerate[1] having over 28 businesses, conducts a healthy in-house competition among their business units for each vertical called 'Pride of Murugappa'. This competition facilitates healthy learning and best practices across the business units which helps them to learn and grow from each business unit.

A business can face challenges at any point in time. But it has to be future-ready despite the challenges. It needs to be geared to face unknown challenges. But how can it be geared without knowing what the challenge is, you may wonder?! *By thinking different, by challenging their own assumptions, beliefs and thought processes and by challenging the status quo, your business can start getting ready to face any unexpected challenges.* This could enable a business to anticipate the unexpected and thereby come up with different possible challenges and suitable solutions to these challenges.

---

[1] Wikipedia. https://en.wikipedia.org/wiki/Murugappa_Group

Thus, the entire management's ability in applying prudence and calculated approach is what would work here.

Watch Out for These Common Mistakes

The common mistakes that businesses commit regarding their future are as follows:

- Not thinking about the future evolution of the business.
- Focusing too much on the short term and missing the big picture.
- Not challenging the status quo.
- Remaining within the comfort zone.
- Not innovating or not reinventing the business.

FINANCIAL GROWTH

While one of the core reasons for the existence of a business is profits, the way a business plans to achieve this should be driven by the purpose. Getting to the root cause and getting to the purpose of each action can help the growth of the business. Similarly, challenging the business processes can also help achieve faster growth. Therefore, it is essential to have answers for the following questions:

- What is the purpose of the business?
- What are the core business values?
- What is the vision of the business?
- What is the mission statement?
- What are the business objectives?

By having these clearly stated, a business has a better sense of direction in the way it needs to be headed and can take the required steps in accomplishing them, which could result in positive financial growth. Like author Simon Sinek says, 'People don't buy what you do, they buy why you do it,' making it important to have your vision and mission statements in place.

If one were to observe large companies, most successful ones are ones with clarity, and they are purpose-driven. For example, the purpose statement of Kellogg's is 'Our Purpose is to nourish families so they can flourish and thrive.'

Similarly, the purpose statement of Nike is 'Our mission is, To bring inspiration and innovation to every athlete* in the world. *If you have a body, you are an athlete.'

The mission statement of Google is 'Our company mission is to organize the world's information and make it universally accessible and useful.'

These statements can be short too, if it conveys the message effectively. For example, for TED, it is 'Spread ideas'.

Ingredients of a good mission statement are as follows:
- Connect with the customer
- Purpose for your people
- Orientation towards your operations

Values can specify the core behaviour of the business such as the kind of experience to be given to the customer, attitude towards suppliers and treatment of employees. These can also include other important aspects such as ethics, integrity, innovation and collaboration. *Will your business compromise values for profits?* Your answer to this question needs to be communicated to all your team members so that all of them are on the same page as you are. There are also good chances that the values that are written and the values that are in actual practice in the organization are not in sync. How is it for your business?

Four Pillars of Strategy

To build an effective strategy for your business, you can build on these four pillars as the basic criteria:

1. Purpose: Know the purpose of your business and build your strategy around it which is in line with your business objectives.
2. Plan: Create your business plans according to the purpose with meticulous thought process by involving the team.
3. Proactive: When the strategy planned is proactive in nature, it is on an ongoing basis to reduce the likelihood of the challenging events of the business.
4. Prioritize: Giving the right priority to the important aspects of your business helps in providing better business insights for the execution of the strategy.

FOUR PILLARS OF STRATEGY

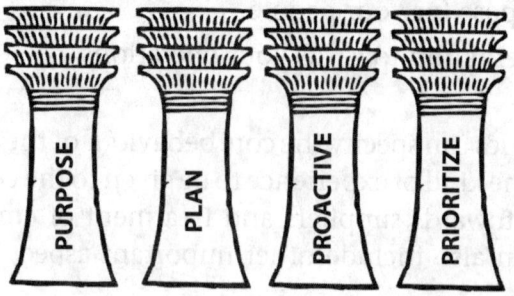

Prepare and Analyse Business Information

Prepare the SWOT (strengths, weaknesses, opportunities and threats) analysis of your business. Update it periodically. Define the uniqueness of your business. What is the edge that you have? How can you convert your threats into opportunities? By defining this strategy, not only to yourself but also the entire team, everyone is aligned and committed to the cause and thereby easy to win over as a team.

The vision, mission, purpose, goals, values, etc., of the business must sync with the ultimate financial objectives. The financial goals should be reviewed along with the business purpose.

Another important question to ask yourself is: 'Are you building your business to grow or are you building it to be sold?' Have clarity and make your business decisions according to your answer. By having the purpose of your business clearly stated, you can plan the path ahead with better clarity in thoughts. This would result in planning the desired actions accordingly.

Watch Out for These Common Mistakes

The common mistakes that businesses commit regarding the business purpose are as follows:

- Not having clearly defined purpose statements.
- Even if the purpose statements exist, these are not communicated to the teams and not given importance to as an organization.
- It is also possible that these statements were defined at the time of inception of the business and thereafter it has become a mere document and everyone knows it exists but no one refers to it.

- Not redefining the purpose statements along with changing times. Missing to revisit and update periodically.
- Failing to understand the importance of the purpose statement.

FINANCIAL PLANNING

The success of a good strategy lies in impeccable implementation, which can result in good financial performance. While planning the overall business strategy, you should also understand the financial needs and financial plan of your business. Especially if your business is looking to grow and scale the financial planning, it becomes important so that your organization can be geared up and meet the requirements.

This calls for meticulous writing of a business plan. You may have all the thoughts collated in your head. However, it is essential to pen them down for better clarity as well as to keep checking progress periodically. By having a business plan in place, you and your team know the way the business needs to be steered ahead. It also acts as a vision board and gives pointers on the way forward. In case you or your team member is lost and carried away by the routine business operations, the business plan serves as a road map and guides the business in what actions should be taken next. It ensures that you are on the desired path of progress. There is no legal requirement to prepare it. However, it is of great benefit for the business to have it documented, especially for future reference.

A business plan is critical in formulating a strategy, understanding the market, checking the feasibility of the project and raising funds, and gives better clarity on the strengths and weaknesses as well as opportunities and threats. It is a good practice to have a business plan in place right at the start of the business and importantly update it at periodic intervals. The plan could also act as a document to convince bankers and help support in funding requirements.

> Food for thought:
> Have you designed the business plan of your business? Even if there is a business plan in place, you need to keep reviewing it and updating it periodically to be in line with the current changing requirements and trends of the business.

Some of the key elements that comprise in the business plan are as follows:

- Executive summary: Expectations of the business to accomplish
- Business description: Key information about the business, including purpose, vision, mission, values, type of customers, nature of operations, goals and so on
- Target market segment along with market expectations
- Competitor analysis: The USP of the business as against competitors
- Details about the offerings (product/service along with value proposition offered)
- Business model (revenue-generation streams, expected margins, financial metrics and related points)
- Marketing plan to reach potential clients and achieve the targets
- People requirement to accommodate the future growth
- Sales strategy along with the plan to sell, sales targets and so on

Based on the above, the financial requirements can be prepared. The numbers need to reflect the following:

- Financial projections: Profit and loss forecast for the next three–five years
- Cash flow forecast: To check if the business is cash-positive or cash-negative
- Request for funding (amount required and the plan for utilization of the funds after considering the overall business progress)

The business plan should be simple, straightforward and practical in terms of adhering to and achieving the stated goals and objectives. It should be prepared after considering the inputs from all the business divisions so that it is exhaustive and the realistic financial requirements are arrived at.

For your business to perform well, your business threats need to be mitigated. The right business principles need to be clarified, and there should be no room for assumptions. As a business owner or a business leader, you need to take the necessary steps to address the following:

- What are your assumptions about your business that need to be removed?
- What measures are in place to protect your business from competition?
- What is the business impact of the decisions that you make in a reflex?
- How secure is your data?
- What is your business fall back?

Like planning the financial requirements, it is essential to plan the resources as well. Resources not just restrict to manpower but also include machinery, capital, office space, etc. These need to be holistic.

Impact on Finance

Apart from the business plan, evaluate the impact each strategy will have on the financial status of your business. Use this to devise ways to overcome challenges.

For example, detailed documentation on the following can be prepared. It must be reviewed periodically and updated.

- If your business is facing stiff competition, devise your competition strategy in such a way that elucidates the plan to capture the market share. The financial impact on competition, as well as the strategy adopted, needs to quantified. If required, a cost–benefit analysis can be prepared.

- Similarly, if your business is dealing with foreign exchange risk and it is affected by currency fluctuations, your foreign exchange strategy should be prepared in such a manner so as to reduce the foreign exchange losses and minimize the uncertainties arising on account of currency fluctuations. It can state if hedging, forward contracts, etc., need to be used and up to what extent, so that this provides required guidance for execution towards the desired objectives.

- If your business relies a lot on digital marketing, then the digital marketing strategy should specify the medium, message, target audience, limits, outcomes, lead generation, conversion, and the upper limit up to which the business is willing to proceed with digital marketing. The financial returns have to be tracked and based on the outcome; the digital marketing strategy needs to be improvised.

Strategies when devised without understanding the financial impact on the business can sometimes prove to be dangerous as all money could be spent, and it is likely that the business could face a cash crunch. Hence, care and caution need to be exhibited.

What happens when there is no strategy nor any planning from the spending perspective? Take the case of Dr Bhargavi who runs Sri Sudhantha Dental Clinic in Vijayawada.

> The clinic was started in rental premises in which she invested heavily in the interiors like fancy ceiling and flooring. When the lease period was completed and they had to move the clinic, she realized that the immovable infrastructure in which they had spent heavily had drained them of their financial resources. Hence, in the new premises, she wisely invested in advanced movable dental equipment, instead of having a grand clinic.

Watch Out for These Common Mistakes

The common mistakes that businesses commit while planning their financial strategy are as follows:

- Missing on the importance of preparing a business plan.
- Not stating the realistic financial requirement—a wish list versus reality. Not being conservative while estimating the financial requirements.
- Overestimating the money in and underestimating the money out.
- Not updating the business plan regularly and in line with the changing business requirements.
- Not assessing the exact progress of the business and not envisaging the real scenario.

FINANCIAL RISK AND DISRUPTION

While thinking and planning on the long-term strategy of your business, consider the financial aspects of your business to plan its growth and to meet its financial requirements in order to scale. However, the risk associated with it is the possible disruption of the industry as well as the potential risk from the competition. Somebody somewhere in the world is working on making your product or service redundant. What can you do about it?

You have to first acknowledge that the world is constantly evolving and that innovations and disruptions have always been happening. Aeroplane, computers, mobiles, etc., have been disruptors at various times. Yet disruption is more spoken about now and is more common. Why? Because the speed of disruption is becoming faster. Disruption was, is and will always be a constant concern for all businesses. Today's business disrupts yesterday's business, and tomorrow's business will disrupt today's. Further, boundaries of industries are blur in this current age where there are digital companies serving as banks, etc.

> Be a disruptor or be ready to get disrupted.

Therefore, you and your business must be cognizant of disruption, especially if you seek growth. How can you be the disruptor in your industry rather than getting disrupted? Do you have the disruption mindset? Challenge your beliefs. Challenge your teams' beliefs. Challenge your assumptions as well as your teams' assumptions. Change your mindset. See your business with a new pair of lenses and a new perspective. How can you create a successful tomorrow and a meaningful future for your business? Think different. And act like never before.

Here is an inspiring story of innovation.

> A commerce graduate homemaker was inspired after a visit to NASA space station in the USA States and wanted more scientists to blossom in India. That is when she got a brain wave to take Indian students to NASA. This idea was ridiculed by many. She fought the odds and on the first trip to NASA in the year 2010, she managed to take 108 children. Since then there is no looking back for Dr Srimathy Kesan, founder of Space Kidz India. This innovative idea in the area of space educational tourism has helped her grow her business manifold and has resulted in revenues and profits more than doubling.

To think like a disruptor, think as if you were to disrupt your own business. For businesses to be disruption-ready, you as the leader need to encourage and facilitate disruptive innovation which will lead to high performance and growth. And to facilitate this, you need to have the strategy well defined as well as the required financial requirements. And more importantly, your team needs to have the freedom to fail in case the disruptive innovation does not work. Because with the teams trying for innovations comes along associated risk, a risk of losing the amount and time spent in the research and development. Hence, from a strategy perspective, separate funds need to be set aside for your business to venture into such disruptive innovations.

While disruption is considered the new normal, it also means looking for other alternatives outside the normal and common ways. So what does it take for your business to be a disruptor?

1. Desire: First, the desire to get better than the present is what will be the driving factor to innovate, disrupt and grow. In most cases, only if a need is felt can the business think about disruption.
2. Vision: Once the desire has sunk in, there needs to be a vision to tread the unknown path ahead. It implies evaluating the possible risks and mitigating them and the means to be successful.
3. Solution: Identify the problem areas that need to be addressed through disruption, based on understating the customer needs. Thereafter, ensure that the right solution can be provided. The solution need not necessarily be an innovation but could also be one that offers convenience and better customer experience and is cost-effective, time-saving, faster and a more efficient way.
4. Potential: Understand the existing business potential in order to implement the desired solution so that the possible issues can be addressed. Further, know the business strengths and evaluate strategies to overcome the weaknesses, which will provide better clarity on how to get better and grow.
5. Challenges: If the initial solution that has been proposed is not working well, then the thinking cap needs to be worn again to ascertain how to overcome challenges and be successful. Grit is required to handle possible failures and keep trying till the right model has evolved. Practical and solution-oriented ways, which clearly state the 'how' of the underlying problem, are what can cause a disruption.

Your business can seek inspiration from a plant that keeps growing despite disruptions. With changing climate, varying water requirements, insects and pests, a plant can get disrupted easily. Yet a plant continues to grow, yield fruits and accomplish its purpose. Disruption in fact makes the plant stronger. Similarly, your business should learn to overcome the different elements of disruption, get stronger, continue to grow and accomplish its business goals.

How can your business handle disruption?

- Purpose: The larger purpose of existence of your business should be clear and the business decisions that are taken should be in line with the identified purpose. With the changing times, the purpose should be evaluated and modified to suit the customer requirements.
- Team: The core team of an organization is what essentially makes the business succeed or crumble. Hence, it is essential that the core team is aligned with the vision of your business and the growth strategy. They need to brainstorm together and think of ways and means to overcome threats and continue to grow. Also essential is to hire the right people who will be aligned to the business vision.
- Expertise: Your business can seek the help of experts, mentors, advisors and coaches and bank on their knowledge and experience to handle disruption and endure growth.
- Financial stability: Undoubtedly, your business has to be financially stable, especially to sustain itself during the testing times of disruption. It would also be essential to set aside cash reserves, which could come in handy to tide over the phase and move in the direction of growth.
- Research and development: It is important to have the required resources to invest in research and development, which can serve as an antidote to disruption and thereby aid growth.
- Technology: We live in the digital era where technology can do wonders. Therefore, your business can leverage technology and take advantage for further growth.

- Security: Safeguarding your business processes with proper security measures in place is vital so that growth is not hindered.

Disruption can be through competition and internal too. Online banking and mobile banking have disrupted the need to have a physical branch of the bank and have enabled growth. Similar is the case with social media marketing, which has disrupted traditional marketing through newspaper advertisements. Your business needs to be geared to face these, be financially prepared along with the associated risks and think differently.

Food for thought:
- If you were to take a sneak peek into the future of your business, how does it look like to you? Go ahead and reimagine the future.
- What would be new? What would be different?
- If you have no constraints and you were to rebuild your business from scratch (in the same domain), how would you go about it?
- If each of your internal functions are to get disrupted one after the other, how will you fix it?

Thus, to keep pace with the changing times, businesses have to embrace disruption, think of unique methods to attract their customers and keep competition at bay, which will result in long-term business growth.

Watch Out for These Common Mistakes

The common mistakes that businesses commit by not thinking about the possible disruption are as follows:

- Being under the false impression that once a leader always a leader of the business.
- Not thinking like a disruptor.
- Not giving the teams the freedom to fail.
- Being under a false notion that disruption cannot happen to their business.
- Lacking the drive to be a disruptor.

Build Your Strategy Action Plan

It is important for you to come up with your strategic plan of action for your business. Some of the actions you can undertake to build your strategy function are stated in the table below.

Rank your current level under each line as Low or Average or Good or Great. Arrive at the desired level and the actions that will get you to the desired level. Measure the financial impact of the action on the top line or bottom line or cash flow. State the non-financial impact of the action. If a topic is not applicable for your business, skip that and move on to the next. To prioritize your action plan, segregate between 'must-have' and 'desirable' actions.

Thoughts for Reflection/Action

- Freeze the vision, mission, goals and objectives of the business, if not done already. Communicate it with the team.
- Brainstorm together with the team on the strategy based on the vision, mission, etc.

S. No.	Topic	Current Level	Proposed Level	Actions To Be Taken	Financial Impact (on Top Line/Bottom Line/Cash Flow)	Non-financial Impact (on Objectives, Vision, Purpose, Teams, etc.)
1	Complete the business model canvas					
2	Formulate a well-defined sales strategy					
3	Well-defined strategies for other important aspects of your business					
4	Level of implementation of existing strategies					
5	Well-defined vision and mission statements					
6	Clearly defined value statements					
7	Communication of the core business objectives to the teams					

(Continued)

S. No.	Topic	Current Level	Proposed Level	Actions To Be Taken	Financial Impact (on Top Line/Bottom Line/Cash Flow)	Non-financial Impact (on Objectives, Vision, Purpose, Teams, etc.)
8	Compilation of SWOT analysis					
9	Business plan review					
10	Financial impact of the different strategies in place					
11	Outcome by challenging your beliefs about your business					
12	Reimagine the future of your business					
13	Question the existing processes					
14	Goals to be communicated to the teams					
15	Design a risk mitigation strategy					

- How much money are you willing to set aside for the business growth for innovation and research?
- Review your business plan on a periodic basis.
- What does it take to grow and scale the business?

LEADERS SPEAK

Nail It to Scale It
Interview of Mr Parthasarathy V. S., President, Mobility Services Sector, and Executive Board Member, Mahindra Group

BUILD TO WITHSTAND

'If you don't know where you are going, you will get nowhere.' This is what makes a strategy important for a business as it gives a direction on how the business should be headed and keeps the business intact of what it is meant to do. A strategy also provides clarity on what is important for the business. It could also be about making a difference.

In the VUCA world that we are in, which is the new normal, it is best to build the business with a blend of innovation and adaptability, which takes into account the business uncertainties in terms of climate change and experiential commerce. Like the boat that functions for a river might not function in the sea, the business models have to change based on the opportunities, risk and related uncertainties so that the business is built to withstand uncertainties.

The elements that need to be integrated into building a business which is meant to withstand should include the following:

- Platform: The right kind of business platform
- Finance options: A mechanism to raise finance at competitive rates including the working capital
- Societal pull: Based on customer preferences such as experiential commerce
- Scale: To breakeven the business first and then strategize to go beyond
- Lastly, the customer experience

State the objectives, how to achieve the objectives and where to get the required resources from, which will build a moat for the business and thereby enhance the success rate. When the thought process of a leader is about getting through the problems, it will enable a mindset shift. Further, while building the business strategically, follow the understated 4S model, which will enable the business to succeed and last. So build the business for the following:

- Survival
- Safety
- Supply chain
- Stability

ROLE OF FINANCE IN STRATEGY

A robust strategy aids in achieving the stated target and, clubbed with the right business goals, will help in better financial performance. If financial performance is not as per the target, check on the reason for the existence of the business and state the business purpose. Good financial performance is contingent on a good strategy.

And a good strategy is one which defines customer experience at the centre and financial performance at the core. The business must make money for all the stakeholders.

In the absence of a chief strategy officer (CSO) or a separate strategy team, the onus is with the chief financial officer (CFO) to plan and prepare the business strategy. The CFO is de facto and de jure as the strategy head and must enable, enhance and engender the business.

STRATEGY IMPLEMENTATION

A clear road map, efficient leadership team and actionable communication enable the smooth implementation of the strategy devised. To execute the strategy, seamlessly follow the following steps, which will lead to financial benefits:

1. Define the policy by the organization head, which states its vision, mission and objectives. For example, when Mahindra started in the mid-20th century, to inculcate high-quality standards up to global levels, the organization's mission was coined as 'Indians are second to none.' A new-age company like Mahindra Logistics defines its purpose as 'Accelerating commerce, empowering communities to rise' and the vision as 'Rise to be an ₹10,000 crore logistics service provider by FY 2026, delivering exceptional customer experience through differentiated, technology enabled solutions.' From this, the yearly business objective including the strategic priorities and projects are identified.

2. The policy that has been crafted has to be deployed to achieve the vision and mission by agreeing with the leadership team.

3. Break the policy deployment into daily management tasks and day-to-day work activity to get to the set objectives and cascade it down to the teams.
4. Use philosophies such as 'Nail it before you scale it' or 'Fire bullets before you fire cannon balls' for execution and customize them so that it will suit specific business needs and provide for improvement and course correction.

ADAPT TO LAST

The strategy should be flexible and not rigid. It should have the sixth sense and a view of what could possibly go wrong with the ability for course correction. The success of every business has four components: strategy, implementation, tenacity and adaptability. It can create a culture of innovation. And culture makes innovation sustainable. In Mahindra, we have defined our culture as 'Accepting no limit, alternative thinking, driving positive change.'

Prepare strategies for various possible business scenarios. Anticipating what can go wrong financially will help for better preparedness, especially in risk mitigation and business not running out of cash. Thus, the measure will be what steps to be taken to overcome the possible challenges. All business risks lead to a financial risk, which will result in financial implications.

A business should be moderate or light and not be asset-heavy. This will help in better adaptability. Build partnerships. Educate teams how to interpret, how to analyse, how to get insight and how the business can learn, so that adaptability becomes easier.

05

BUILDING FINANCIAL EFFICIENCY IN OPERATIONS

CORE OF THE OPERATIONS FUNCTION: OUTPUT ORIENTED BY ORGANIZING OPTIMALLY

A pulp mill company founded in the year 1865 in Finland started expanding its business operations into manufacturing of toilet papers, then to tyres, electrical power generation and telephones. Eventually, it had spun off most of its operations except its telecommunications business. This business helped pioneer the mobile industry, and thus Nokia became the largest mobile phone maker in the world in the late 1990s.[1]

Samsung[2] started originally as a trading company in 1938, while LG Corporation's early products were soaps and toothpaste.[3]

---

[1] Wikipedia. https://en.wikipedia.org/wiki/Nokia

[2] Wikipedia. https://en.wikipedia.org/wiki/Samsung

[3] Wikipedia. https://en.wikipedia.org/wiki/LG_Corporation

These are some of the well-known stories in business, wherein there was a total shift in the business operations where these companies emerged as leaders during the course of their business. But there are many more stories of businesses that did not make it successful in shifting their business operations into a different industry. They only ended up losing money while trying their hands at different operations.

The success of the strategy developed depends on the execution and implementation. To ensure success in your business, it needs a strong operations team, who can foresee all aspects of the business operations right from facilities management to customer management to integration and diversification. Business operations are those activities that will enhance the value of the business and also facilitate profit. Hence, a lot of care and caution need to be exhibited in managing it efficiently.

As the business owner/head, you need to understand and work on the following:

- What are the business operations that are required to support the growth of the business?
- What are the products or services that your business is rendering which is adding financial value to your business?
- How is your business adding value to your customer?

Some organizations do not have a specific person to manage the operations. These could be rolled under the chief executive officer or the business head. This call can be taken depending on the need and size of the business operations. The main point is that there must be a person in charge of and responsible to run the business operations efficiently and be in a position to overcome the business bottlenecks for the smooth operations of your business.

The business operations function has to ensure the following:

- Smooth designing and implementation of the operations of the business
- Establishing policies that promote organization culture, vision and mission
- Overseeing the business operations and ensuring coordination and delivery

Figure 5.1. Profit Hack Wheel of the Operations Function

The intersection of business operations and finance is value creation—creating value for the customers as well as for the business, thereby having a win-win situation. Let us explore the following in this chapter:

1. What is the investment required for smooth running and expansion of your business operations?
2. What are the financial operational metrics to focus upon?

3. What is the impact of time on your business operations and the related financial implications?
4. What are the financial efficiencies of your business operations?

The answers to the above questions are collated together and are represented as the profit hack wheel of the operations function in Figure 5.1.

INVESTMENT FOR BUSINESS OPERATIONS

In the huge office complex in the heart of the city, a well-funded tech start-up which was about 3 years old and had over 50 employees had a very plush and swanky office. It had the latest facilities for its employees, ranging from sports facilities to transport facilities. It also offered free sumptuous food for its employees on every working day.

The employees of the adjacent organization within the same building, which was in business for over 20 years, were jealous of the employees working for the start-up, because of these fancy offerings, and they often compared it with the facilities that were provided in their organization. Ironically, it did not provide them anything as fancy as the tech start-up.

This decision of giving fancy perks, bonuses, etc., varies from organization to organization. While some businesses shun it, other businesses embrace such matters. The decision varies on many aspects but is mainly dependent on the financial situation of the business—whether it can afford such benefits for its employees or not. When it comes to your business, apart from the financial feasibility, investing and spending on fancy items depend on your views, your organizational values, goals and aspects like nature of the business operations, thought process of the leadership team, industry trends, salaries given, etc. I would also like to draw your attention to the concept of return on expense, which was discussed in Chapter 1. Based on these various parameters, you can decide the extra expenses you want to continue with and the ones to let go.

For smooth business operations, investment is also required in the form of assets for employees such as laptops and mobiles. Many organizations are moving away from this traditional method to BYOD (Bring your own device). However, what you have to be wary of in such cases is the data leakage, safety and security of your business information. Of course, the people wanting to commit fraud will anyway find a way out. Should you decide to provide your team with these assets, note that the impact on the profit will only be to the extent of the depreciation. Cash flow impact will be there. Irrespective of which method you chose, the point is that you need to come out with ways that would work well for your business and ensure timely and excellent delivery to your customers.

Capacity utilization of resources plays an important role in business operations. By understanding the nuances of your business, you can navigate your way towards better profits. Here is the story of Jothi Shankar of GoTek, which is into manufacturing lanyards.

Unlike the smaller players in the industry, GoTek had invested in a high-end manufacturing equipment, which had the capacity to manufacture one lakh lanyards at one go. However, the utilization of the equipment was only at 20 per cent initially. When Shankar realized the play of marginal costing on production, he increased the capacity utilization to 50 per cent. This gave him the power to offer lowered pricing to his customers, winning competition, and that helped in the revenue and profit growth of the business.

Business Expansion

Further, from a business operations' perspective, you could evaluate options such as mergers and acquisitions (M&As) and the related financial implications. These decisions can be made depending on the purchasing power of your business. Such decisions have their pros and cons. While it may be good from a business expansion point of view, the challenge could be in managing the employees, defining processes, smooth knowledge transfer, etc. There have been many instances of takeover such as Google acquiring Android and Walt Disney acquiring Marvel, as well as cases of hostile takeovers like Larsen & Toubro takeover of Mindtree. Nonetheless, whatever be the type of merger or acquisition, there needs to be a strong leadership team to handle the M&A and build a strong company culture for getting the best from the teams.

For better facilitation of business operations, other choices can also be forward or backward integration. Forward integration is by merging or acquiring a distributor or retailer, whereas backward integration is by merging with the supplier of the manufacturer.

Here is a checklist of some key questions that you need to ask before deciding on the merger or acquisition or integration:

- How would this merger or acquisition or integration contribute to the financial growth of your business?

- What are the synergies that will be available? How does the culture match?
- What is the modus operandi of the transaction?
- Has sufficient due diligence been done?
- What will be the ratio of the new shareholding?
- What is the total cost of acquisition? How can you source this amount?
- How will the money invested be recovered?
- What is the time duration to recover the money invested? (also called the payback period)
- What are the exit clauses (should the merger not work well at a later date, for whatever reasons)?

Similarly, when diversifying the business operations, a well-thought-out, conscious and clear business decision needs to be made, which will help the business to propel forward.

Remember that while much is spoken about mergers, demergers are also not uncommon. You could demerge or spin off a particular business vertical for various reasons such as increasing global footprint, restructuring of the business and tax benefits.

Watch Out for These Common Mistakes

The common mistakes that businesses commit regarding the investment for business operations are as follows:

- Not anticipating potential threats.
- Not challenging the regular process of business operations.
- Not having a detailed plan for smooth integration in case of an M&A.

Basis for Acquisition

According to Mr Raghunandana Tangirala, Managing Director of UDS Facility Services which acquired Matrix Business Services, there are no fixed rules as such for an acquisition. It varies depending on the acquiring company's strategy. Normally, each acquiring company sets out a rule book based on their business strategy on aspects such as:

- Why make an acquisition?
- What does the business and the acquiring company have in common?
- Does this align with the overall business strategy?

The different reasons for the companies to acquire include economies of scale, market share, better synergy, cost reduction, to gain geography, to reduce supply, to decrease competition, to leverage technology, etc. The reason can also be when the current business is lacking some advantages and finds that the target business can complete that shortfall.

That apart, some important points other than business strategies for a successful acquisition are as follows:

- Do both the businesses have a common core to build on?
- Do both the businesses have a similar cultural fit and value systems?
- Does it benefit both the businesses?

Numbers alone should not be the influencing factors for the decisions. Weightage has to be given for quality rather than quantity.

A successful acquisition must clearly and rapidly create visible opportunities for advancement for both organizations. Most of the time, it's the people who are just as crucial as the widget or service they offer. State explicitly how the acquisition will benefit the people in the business as well as the acquiring business.

The best time to opt for an acquisition is when 'need meets opportunity'. From his or her experience, one can claim that the right time for a company to seek acquisition is when

- There is a need to build and scale faster.
- The industry is consolidating due to various reasons.
- It can quickly create competitive advantage/entry barriers.
- The acquisition can quickly add better value for both the organizations.
- Acquisition enhances technology or business service expansion to retain/improve the market standing.

Normally, M&As are successful in similar lines of business. However, if the strategy is to diversify the existing business or offer a different portfolio of products/services, then considering a diverse business acquisition could be more difficult and therefore has to have an elaborate plan, strategy and management bandwidth.

In our case, UDS's strategy was to transform into an integrated business support services company rather than be a pure play facilities management business. In addition to this strategy, UDS also wanted a short/medium-term arbitrage before it goes public.

- Not having clarity or not specifying the growth path ahead.
- Not being prepared to meet the financial requirements in case of an emergency.
- Inability to handle the transition and the changed management.

FINANCIAL METRICS FOR SCALING

For a business to scale up, there could be umpteen ways. However, it is essential for you to define the key financial metrics that are important for your business growth. Let me explain this with an example.

> A large manufacturing company was desirous of growth. Over the span of two years, they almost doubled the production. Sales grew by 70 per cent. Everyone in the organization was focused on sales growth. They acquired new customers and were also considering penetrating into new markets. While this was the positive side of the story, the flip side was that the business had failed to retain existing customers; the value of their stock in hand was high; their cash collections were poor; and the concept of working capital management did not exist. While the profit grew in absolute terms compared to the previous years, the percentage of profit was lesser as they had spent a lot on marketing and other related expenses.

Take a moment's pause and reflect if this is the kind of growth that you need for your organization. *Define your key financial metrics.* Remember that while scaling up, it is essential to define the processes, policies and procedures so that the growth does not blur the basics. Where do you want your business to focus on? What are your key financial metrics with respect to the anticipated growth? Set these metrics, and communicate them with your team so that the entire team is working towards the same.

Here is an example of an entrepreneur who had defined his key financial metric on operational profits rather than revenue growth.

> Sagar Makwana, of JyoAsh Engineers, is into manufacturing automobile components for two-wheelers. He says that he was quick to realize that one of the products manufactured had a lower selling price but higher profit compared to another product that he manufactured which had a higher selling price but lower profit. Therefore, he reached out to his customers pushing for the sale of the product with better margins, even though it meant that his turnover would not be as high. This thought process was different compared to his competitors, which helped his profits to grow.

Some food for thought for you from both the operational and financial perspectives:
- If your business is intending to go global, then what sort of tie-ups or partners are you seeking?
- Will your business be only into services or only products or a combination of the two?
- How can your business cater to the demands of the potential customers?

Along with the growth come unexpected challenges. How geared is your business to face them? Take baby steps in getting your business organized for new challenges together with your team. The potential risks that you foresee with the scaled operations need to be mitigated and necessary actions to be taken in that regard.

You can also customize a specific financial dashboard for measuring the growth and performance of your business. This will give you an immediate picture of how the business is doing at one glance.

Why–Why Analysis

For a business to plan its operations effectively and efficiently, performing the why–why analysis could be a good analytical method. It is designed to help identify the factors that contribute to a problem and derive the root cause for failure. It is an interrogative technique to explore the cause and effect of an underlying business problem. It works on the principle of using 'why' as a repeated question. It was first used in Toyota Motor Corporation.

According to Mr Raghavan Neelakantan, President, Lucas Indian Service of the TVS Group, most start-up founders and entrepreneurs are very sure what product or service they would offer to the market. However, it's important for them to do a why–why analysis of their idea which would provide better clarity for efficient operations. Answering the questions below will clarify the need to know the customer profile to create a product/service:

- Why would a customer buy the product?
- What problem does it solve?
- Is the customer aware of the problem?
- If so, how is the customer managing the situation?
- What are the available alternatives for the customer?

- Is the customer simply deciding to put up with the problem?

Then the customer is defined in flesh, blood and warmth. Profiling the customer further will help to understand why the customer would buy. What would be the customer's expectations? What experience will make the customer satisfied, happy or delighted?

These questions together will solve the quality and production puzzle, and the operations can be planned in accordance. In order to delight the customer, the customer's total experience needs to be carefully designed. The entrepreneur would then know what role the product or service plays by itself, and what role the interfaces play. This is the first step in creating a customer-driven quality management programme and production system for efficient operations.

Once the customer profile is defined and is not an amorphous 'category', the entrepreneur would know how many such profiles can be decided to reach out to and create a demand. This would help calculate the operational efforts required.

This process would help in clarifying any potential disruption in the industry. How will the respective industry react? Who will disrupt and by when? Hence, arrive at what's the shelf life of the product or service.

Once the competitive landscape is defined, the entrepreneur would know the extent of opportunity that exists and the risks thereof and the associated rewards. This would then help the entrepreneur focus on how much money is needed.

Getting money for a viable idea is relatively easy. Not frittering away, the funding is difficult. Financial prudence needs to complement passion and innovation.

The advantages in using this analysis include the following:

- Identifying the root cause of the problem
- Systematic problem-solving
- Easy and effective to use
- Incorporates a culture of continuous development

Watch Out for These Common Mistakes

The common mistakes that businesses commit regarding the financial metrics that are important for the business operations are as follows:

- Not defining the key financial metrics of the business.
- Not communicating the financial metrics to the team.
- Focusing only on the top-line growth and neglecting the bottom-line impact.
- Not giving importance to free cash flow reserves.
- Not thinking about the financial aspects needed for growth.
- Not linking the KRAs with financial growth of the business.

TIME FACTOR

Time has a value to it. Time is money and also an invisible cost. Many businesses fail to take the time factor into account, thinking time to be a free resource and unlimited. Interest charges, depreciation and time value of money are all examples of the impact time has on your business from a financial perspective.

Project delays, not delivering on time or rework costs, all have the effect of time, resulting in financial implications which erode the profit. Hence, the business operations need to take into account all the aspects relating to time and the associated risks.

> A car-manufacturing company was dependent on a particular supplier for a specific part of the car. This supplier was in turn dependent on another specific smaller supplier for the supply for a customized part, which was crucial and exclusive in the manufacture of the said part. The production of this precise design of this particular part takes a minimum of two months. This supplier for the car company did not have an alternate supplier, as they were dealing with this supplier for many years. What they missed was that should there be any unforeseen delay or stoppage from the small supplier, the main supplier to the car would get impacted, in turn impacting the manufacture of the car. Neither the car manufacturer nor their supplier could foresee this potential threat to the business operations till they got affected. It was a lesson that was learnt the hard way.

For time-consuming processes like these, alternate plans should be in place so that the business operations are not affected, as these sort of delays ultimately impact the financial position, apart from the loss of market reputation.

Food for thought:
When was the last time you did something new to reduce the processing time involved? Trying new things and different ways as against the set norms will help you discover newer and shorter ways to do the same thing.

Rex Aantonny, the founder of Rex Cyber Solutions which is an independent information security consultancy based in Chennai, took a difficult business decision. The business was working on many small projects which were of little value. These projects were time-consuming and offered poor margins. Hence, the business decision which was taken was that only projects above a certain threshold would be worked upon, creating value-based outcomes for their client. Initially, this was a big constraint and the revenue dipped. However, through word of mouth, the high-paying clients referred Rex Cyber Solutions to their contacts, and the business grew. Within a span of six months, their profits doubled.

Thus, for an organization, it is essential to plan and manage the time on its business operations and benefit from it. Also, it would be effective to compute ways and means by which time taken for the operations can be reduced in order to gain financially.

Competitor Analysis

Competition is common for all businesses. For your business to be on top of the game, it is essential to know what your competitors are up to. By knowing that, you can decide on how you want to play your business game and grow your profits. Timely action is crucial for the successful implementation of your competition strategy.

To strengthen your business from the competition, you need to build an economic moat. ('An economic moat is a distinct advantage a company has over its competitors which allows it to protect its market share and profitability. It is often an advantage that is difficult to mimic or duplicate (brand identity, patents) and thus creates an effective barrier against competition from other firms.'[4])

By devising a competitor analysis framework, it will help you not only in your decision-making and making required business changes but also in knowing where your business stands and benchmark your performance against the competitors. Plan your business operations action after considering the same.

A sample of a framework for competitor analysis is shared below, which you can customize as per your requirements.

Watch Out for These Common Mistakes

The common mistakes that many businesses do regarding the time factor of the business operations are as follows:

- Not thinking about the time factor.
- Not knowing that time is a hidden cost.
- Reluctance and resistance in trying newer and less time-consuming ways. (An example of this is on business travel. There used to be reluctance and resistance to virtual meetings initially. However, post COVID, meetings happen virtually rather seamlessly).
- Failing to think about time constraints.
- Thinking that time is unlimited for the business.
- Not devising ways to reduce the process cycle time.

---

[4] Investopedia.com. https://www.investopedia.com/terms/e/economic moat.asp

	Your Business	Competitor 1	Competitor 2	Competitor 3	Operational Action Plan
Yearly turnover					
Cost of sales/cost of production					
Profit margin					
Market share					
No. of employees					
Major customers					
Major suppliers					
Strengths					
Weaknesses					
Opportunities					
Threats					
Advertising agency					
Auditors					
Produce features					
Top-selling product					
USP					

No. of dealerships				
Discounts offered				
Debtors' collection cycle				
Daily production				
Asset turnover ratio				
Debt equity ratio				

FINANCIAL EFFICIENCIES

Financial efficiency means how the amount invested in each operation is yielding revenue to the business. How the money that you have invested in the business is churning around and contributing to the business growth? This is especially applicable if you are offering a wide range of products and (or) services. Check on aspects like the following:

- What is the vertical-wise/department-wise/product-wise/service-wise profitability?
- How can the process length be reduced?
- How can wastages (in processes, in material, time taken, etc.) be kept minimal?
- What can be done differently in the business operations to reduce costs?
- What are the different parameters (such as cost per employee, revenue per employee and contribution per item) indicating? How can it be improved?

Let me give you an example of a company dealing in IT services. The company was wanting to build its niche in a particular segment in the IT industry. It was striving to make its mark in that particular domain. While this business vertical was successful, the business had challenges in getting the right candidates due to the niche and that salaries were very high. It was making around 10 per cent margin in this vertical. Another of the IT service rendered was providing not only better margin of 20 per cent, but volumes were also growing and there was tremendous potential to grow this vertical even further.

So the company was facing a dilemma of which one to focus on. Whether in building its specific niche and settle for lesser profits or go full on on the other vertical? After much thought, the company gave itself a time frame for growth in the domain where it was seeking a niche, failing which it decided to specialize exclusively in the other service domain from a financial perspective. In such situations, market research and customer survey on preferences and expectations could help gauge whether the market is indeed ready immediately or in near future for the niche product/service.

Business decisions need to be made by carefully weighing the pros and cons. Of course, the decisions need not be only from a financial perspective. For example, you may consider servicing a particular client with even low margins probably because you think that it is a good brand to have in your client portfolio and may want to leverage more sales through it. *The important aspect is taking decisions where you are fully aware of the financial repercussions.* The key to note here is that while striving for financial efficiencies, there should be no compromise on quality and delivery schedules.

Gemba Kaizen

Kaizen is a Japanese concept, which means continuous improvement for enhancing processes and reducing waste. In Japanese, Gemba means the real place. Within the lean context, Gemba refers to the place where the value is created, and Kaizen denotes the improvements. What are the ways and means by which your business operations can be improved? Reflect on the following founding principles of Kaizen, which could provoke your thoughts for your business operations to improve:

- Teamwork
- Personal discipline
- Better morale
- Quality circles
- Ways to improve

The golden rules of Gemba are as follows:

- Go to the place (Gemba) first.
- Check the defect (*Gembutsu*, a Japanese word for the real thing).
- On-the-spot temporary counter-measures to be taken.
- Find out the root cause.
- Standardize operations to prevent recurrence.

You can adopt these Japanese principles to enhance the efficiency levels of your business operations, which will translate into better financial results. Having standard operating procedures across your organization will help. Similarly, if you have different locations/branches of your business, ensure that the operations are set at the levels as expected. Should you detect a procedure that is incorrectly followed at any of the locations, check for the same mistake at other locations as well and adopt preventive measures.

Operations Improvement Matrix

You can use the sample matrix template given below if you would like to improve the business operations by comparing what went well and what can be improved.

How you can work on this matrix:

1. Take the period which you want to improve. (It can be the next month, next quarter or next year.)
2. Compare the performance for a similar/adjacent period. (Remember to compare apples to apples.)

3. Assess in the current period what went well and what did not. In the example below, the entrepreneur has assessed what was unfavourable—the inventory was not managed well in the current year but had the potential to improve. Similarly, as per the entrepreneur's assessment, the research and development of the new product was not favourable in the current year but had the potential to grow in the next year.

4. In the example, what was favourable for the entrepreneur in the current year was that the production capacity was utilized to its peak and therefore it was found that there was scope to operate in shifts to increase the production in the next year.

5. Prepare your matrix for your next period, based on the current period, on what was favourable and unfavourable with the potential to grow and improve.

6. Build your action plan around it.

| | | Current Year | |
		Unfavourable	Favourable
Next Year	Potential to grow	R&D for new product	Production capacity
	Potential to improve	Inventory management	Operate in shifts

Watch Out for These Common Mistakes

The common mistakes that businesses commit regarding the financial efficiency of business operations are as follows:

- Not setting measures to calculate the financial efficiency of the business operations.

S. No.	Topic	Current Level	Proposed Level	Actions To Be Taken	Financial Impact (on Top Line/Bottom Line/Cash Flow)	Non-financial Impact (on Team, Processes, Efficiency, etc.)
1	Ways to improve capacity utilization					
2	Evaluate expansion possibilities					
3	Key financial metrics of your business					
4	Key business decisions based on product-wise/vertical-wise profit-ability					
5	Revisit the financial dashboard to include the month-on-month progress					
6	Outcome of the why–why analysis					
7	Evaluate ways to curtail the process/cycle time					
8	Decisions based on the competition scorecard					

9	Key outcomes from the operations improvement matrix			
10	Plug loopholes and gaps in the operation systems.			
11	Outcome by challenging your beliefs about your business			
12	Strategize different ways to improve the quality of your product or service			
13	Ways to avoid/minimize delays and rework costs			
14	Ideate and repackage current ways of operation procedures			
15	Update your business continuity plan (BCP) as well as your disaster recovery plan (DRP)			

- Not interpreting the business impact of financial calculations.
- And if the calculations are prepared, not analysing the impact of the numbers.
- Failing to think of the financial implications for the business decisions.
- Not working on ways to improve the financial efficiency of the business operations.

Build Your Operations Action Plan

Business operations need to be smooth to ensure business continuity. Hence, you need to take the required steps for hassle-free business operations. Listed below are few actions that you can take in this regard.

Rank your current level under each line as Low or Average or Good or Great. Arrive at the desired level and the actions that will get you to the desired level. Measure the financial impact of the action on the top line or bottom line or cash flow. State the non-financial impact of the action. If a topic is not applicable for your business, skip that and move on to the next. To prioritize your action plan, segregate between 'must-have' and 'desirable' actions.

Thoughts for Reflection/Action

- Define the key financial metrics which are crucial for your business operations.
- Prepare a hypothetical scenario of the financial impact of time and project delays in your business.

- What are the various ways in which the processes of your business operations can be reduced significantly?
- List the various possibilities of challenges to your business operations along with the preventive measures.
- What can be your instant remedies for unexpected challenges in business operations?

LEADERS SPEAK

Focus Is the Key
Interview of Mr C. K. Ranganathan, Chairman, CavinKare

EXPANSION OF BUSINESS OPERATIONS

A company's financial muscle, ability to invest and leadership capabilities determine whether the business should have a niche business offering or offer a range of products and services. If only one person has to do it all, there is a limitation and they cannot spread themselves too thin. However, if there are independent business houses that operate as strategic business units, then the business can expand its operations. It will make the business more focused. At CavinKare, we have special business units and exclusive leadership teams managing the entire range of our offerings. For businesses that are looking to expand their operations, they need to know their bandwidth before taking the plunge.

CavinKare offers both products as well as services and is able to manage because of the specialists who have managed to build the services business from scratch.

Each of our business units is self-sufficient, has its own vision and mission, generates cash and is independent in its operations.

BUSINESS PERFORMANCE VERSUS FINANCIAL PERFORMANCE

Financial performance is a subset of the overall business performance. When financial performance is healthy, the business will be on the healthier side. While the financial performance only features financial stability, the business performance is a holistic indicator. Monitoring business performance (which includes financial performance) is a great way to manage a business. Apart from specific business nuances, few common financial parameters are top-line growth, EBITDA margins, benchmarking against competition and working capital. The various non-financial parameters such as product edge, economic moat, innovation quotient and business health scorecard are ways to monitor the business performance.

At CavinKare, we have adopted the five-second compelling scorecard, which is similar to the cricket scorecard. It displays whether the business team is winning or losing. It conveys the story within five seconds on specific business parameters. Upon reviewing it, the individual members themselves know that there is a need to take corrective actions.

Business unit-wise, stock-wise, market-wise, product-wise, state-wise and customer segment-wise profitability needs to be monitored to know the exact business story. Sometimes despite low vertical profitability, at CavinKare we deliberately allow the performance because of the high trajectory of growth to acquire market share. Based on this, we decide to either increase the price or lower the cost of production or cost of operations as the case may be. Comparing performance with competition and knowing how the business scores against the competition should be a yardstick for the business. The bottom line reflects on the health of the business. Along with profitable growth, the business should also focus on growing the market share.

Input-based responsibility rather than output-based responsibility should be inculcated within the business. Efficiency will be higher when certain roles are outsourced that are monotonous and routine in nature and that do not add extra value.

EXECUTION CAPABILITIES

Instead of getting caught up in the day-to-day firefighting activities, the business should focus on working towards their strategy, vision and mission, which should be focused towards achieving the business goals and objectives. Based on the strategy to achieve the objectives, the operational plan can be devised. A business can have great ideas, but if it does not have good execution capabilities, then there is no use. That is what makes it important for a business to invest in great culture, team development, leadership, learning and development, etc. Investing and building human capital are extremely important. Continuously developing capabilities to lead the company is essential. A strong human capital can contribute to the financial growth and will come out with flying colours rather than with suboptimal human capital.

At the same time, the business should not ignore technology. By having the ability to foresee the future, leveraging on technology and how the customers will change enables a business to be a disruptor.

FORWARD OR BACKWARD INTEGRATION

While evaluating the forward integration or backward integration decisions, some of the key points for consideration by the business are as follows:

- Whether the business has extra cash to spare
- If it is a good business opportunity
- Inability to handle the competition
- Need to increase market share
- Getting into adjacent areas in the value chain
- Reduction in cost of production
- Insufficient innovation
- Leadership struggles

Apart from the above, the culture, capability of execution and current financial strength will be good bases to evaluate. However, if there is enough on the plate, then it is better not to resort to integration because the focus should not be diluted. Focus is the key.

06

FINANCIAL RETURNS FROM MARKETING

CORE OF THE MARKETING FUNCTION: MINDFUL MESSAGE TO THE MARKET THROUGH RIGHT MEDIA

If you want the bottom line of your business to grow, then marketing is a great channel to enable business profits. It helps in showcasing your products and services to your potential clients, thereby facilitating revenue growth.

Many people do not like marketing, as they feel that it is a way of bragging. There are others who think that they do not need marketing or undermine the importance of marketing because they feel that they are leaders in their domain or expect that the customers reach out to them. For the people with the former view, how will people know about the products or services that you are offering? And for the latter, even though your business may be the market leader, if you want to continue to be on top of the mind of your customers, it is essential to leverage on marketing. Through marketing, your business identifies the customers' needs and determines how best to meet the needs of the customer.

Marketing could be in the form of digital marketing, advertising, promotions, branding, email marketing, search engine optimization, content marketing, etc. And it has to be in line with the current times. Take for example the creative advertisement by Cadbury for the biggest festival of India—Diwali. What is special about an advertisement you may wonder. The advertisement was conceptualized by Ogilvy, which has used artificial intelligence to advertise the local retailers whose business has been affected by the pandemic. It goes with the title of 'Not Just a Cadbury Ad'.[1] This ad became a talking point because of some reasons listed below:

- Hyper-personalized marketing by custom-designing the same advertisement based on pin codes and the geographic location of the viewer
- Was a unique and innovative concept of not just advertising for itself
- Leveraged on digital and technology by creating a unique and real-time data experience
- Collaborated with the local vendors, thus creating a win–win situation
- Created goodwill and branding for itself
- Connected well and resonated with customers
- Improved brand visibility
- Enabled the growth of local small vendors

While traditionally marketing is considered an expense, if a business plays well on marketing, it can help enable boost the top line and thereby the bottom line of the business. In this section of marketing, let us check on the following aspects:

---

[1] https://www.youtube.com/watch?v=gBWLm6Sx1WI

1. How can marketing be leveraged to enhance the top-line growth?
2. How can marketing be cost-effective?
3. How to handle the financial threats in marketing?
4. What are the parameters for considering ROI on marketing?

The answers to the above questions are collated together and are represented as the profit hack wheel of the marketing function in Figure 6.1.

Figure 6.1. Profit Hack Wheel of the Marketing Function

GROWING THE TOP LINE THROUGH MARKETING

The function of marketing is a key lever for growing the sales of a business. It is a means to let the potential customers know about what is being offered by your business which will make the life of the customer easy. Thus, it is a good way to lure the customer into buying by creating a feeling of demand for the product or service. Effective communication to the customer enables the customer to understand the need for buying your product or service.

While the marketing function can be easily described as above, the big question is: How to get your potential customers to buy? There are some brands that do an excellent job of marketing, but the product may not be of the said quality, thus leaving a bad taste for the customer. The customer feels cheated. This results not only in the loss of customers but also loss of brand reputation which a business has to be extra cautious of. For the sake of short-term sales, both the long-term image and reputation are lost.

It is essential to step into the shoes of the customer to understand what their pain points are. Having a regular and repeated channel of communication enables being constantly in touch with the customer for them to connect with your product or service and more so your company. It is said that out of sight is out of mind. Therefore, communication becomes essential. Further establishing the relatability with the customer is important. For example, a large company spent a huge amount on marketing and used a foreign model. It fell flat because subconsciously the customers felt that it was not for them as they were unable to connect with the product.

A lot of the growth through marketing depends on the right channel used to reach out to the customers. And it is essential to be upfront about what it offers, for whom, benefits, etc. For example, Saregama's Carvaan (similar to traditional radio in a contemporary avatar) clearly mentioned that the product is not targeted for Gen Y or Gen Z.

For your marketing initiatives to work well, remember that the value proposition to the prospect must be conveyed effectively. What is the edge that your business has over competitors? Why should anyone enter into a business deal with you? What are the benefits of using your product or services? Have clear answers to these while starting your marketing campaign.

Impact from Referral Marketing

Can a business grow without marketing? Of course there are instances.

> Continuing with the above example of Carvaan, they did not have a fancy nationwide launch nor spent on huge advertisements. They relied on audio vehicles such as radio and podcast for the initial push. Thereafter, they picked up with the dealers and mainly through word of mouth, which created higher demand. This was possible because they were able to identify that this resonated with their target audience and there was a void in that space despite having many music channels and gadgets. This product also created an emotional connect with the customer that they did not have to spend much on marketing it.

It was more of a pull marketing than push marketing.

When there is a happy customer, a business gets more customers through referrals and word of mouth. Be it a restaurant, movie, book or any product, if the customer has gained by it or has had a delightful experience, they would share with their family, friends, colleagues, etc. They become the biggest brand ambassadors for your business. Some businesses also offer a commission or a flat amount or a discount to customers who have referred another customer for their business. Referral is a good way to get the top line to grow.

Referrals also work in businesses which seek new talent. When employees refer another person who is absorbed into the company, the existing employees get a referral bonus.

Give this a thought: What are the possible ways you can get your business to grow through referrals?

Impact of Digital Marketing

As against the traditional marketing, which was through newspapers, TV advertisements, radio channels, etc., in this digital era, when the marketing is done through digital medium, digital marketing is a big boon and is cost-effective compared to the traditional marketing. It allows you to carefully choose your exact target audience and reach out only to them as you can specify the profile, segment, age group, gender, interests, etc.

Here is an interesting example of how a business has taken an enormous leap because of the digital route.

Siddharth Rajasekar is the founder of Internet Lifestyle Hub, creating a community for digital coaches and mentors. He does not have an office nor full-time employees. Instead, he works with a few freelancers. He has managed to grow significantly. This was possible as he placed regular advertisements on Facebook and targeted his exact audience. The cost of his lead conversion keeps varying, and he has a constant eye on this cost.

Take another instance of Puneet Rao, a fitness trainer.[2] During the lockdown due to the coronavirus pandemic, he earned ₹24 lakh in 24 hours! How was this possible? He used digital means and did not spend anything significant on marketing. His strategy was simple. He leveraged on his huge followers on Instagram. He offered free online fitness classes for three weeks, thereby letting his customers get a feel of what it was like. Thereafter, he launched his online fitness course at ₹2,000 per month and had over 1,200 people who signed up for it as soon as he opened it up for payments, and his revenue just grew. With no location constraints, he is now earning more than the pre-lockdown days. His posts are not just about fitness but also about his family, thus creating a connect with his audience.

The Facebook advertisement placed by Slack caught the eye of many because of the effective messaging.[3] It read –'What it feels like to sit in 25% fewer meetings' with the tag line 'Slack: Make work better'. The picture that went with it in this advert was also an attractive one. Therefore, the entire packing needs to be presented well for the advert to be effective in digital.

Watch Out for These Common Mistakes

The common mistakes that businesses commit regarding the marketing plan for top-line growth are as follows:

- Not addressing the 'What's in it for me' for the potential customer.

---

[2] https://www.shreyapattar.com/linked-in-post/he-made-%E2%82%B92400000-%E2%82%B924-lacs-in-24-hrs/

[3] https://www.wordstream.com/blog/ws/2016/05/23/facebook-ad-examples

- Not being upfront about how the customer can get benefited by the products' features.
- Not leveraging on the USP of the product or service.
- Failing to follow up on potential leads.
- Not clearly defining the target audience or not marketing to the decision-makers in a large organization.

COST-EFFECTIVE MARKETING

The examples given above of the fitness trainer Puneet and of Carvaan are examples of cost-effective marketing, also known as *frugal marketing*. How did they manage to do cost-effective marketing? If we were to analyse them further, we can notice the following patterns:

- Having a unique factor
- Solving a need for the customer
- Building a brand
- Establishing credibility
- Creating a connect with the customers
- Ensuring there is a high trust quotient
- Having the right audience
- Connecting through emotions
- Right pricing leading to a huge volume
- Keeping it simple—no-nonsense approach
- Referrals from existing customers
- Customizing the product or service for the audience

Therefore, marketing need not be expensive but can be frugal. The key from a finance angle is that whatever is the amount spent on marketing, it must be recovered manifold, which is what makes it worthwhile for a business.

One of the cheapest and effective ways to market is content marketing. It is done typically online by engaging social media posts, videos, blogs, etc. It does not explicitly promote the product or service but is intended to stimulate interest in the offerings. It focuses on creating, publishing and distributing content to the target audience online. An example of content marketing includes Coke's 'Share a Coke' campaign.

Impact from Outlier Marketing

Outlier marketing is another effective way, wherein as a business what you do must get the required ROI. Outlier marketing is a frugal manner which provokes you and encourages you to use what you have within and around you, using the existing ideas and instruments which can be repurposed and used.

Outlier marketing deviates from the norm, thereby giving a high stickiness quotient, resulting in higher recall value. It relies on agile and frugal marketing techniques to get the desired outcomes. In other words, if you are selling apples, you need to be the red apple among the green apples, so that you stand out. What is your point of differentiation?

Be different and stand out. (Just like this box on this page, which gets your attention!) When the way you do your business is different, your business is talked about, thereby getting the required attention and branding. What are you known for? Create the curiosity factor.

Outlier marketing capitalizes on ideas such as conducting online contests, leveraging through LinkedIn connections, seeking collaborations, email marketing, instructional videos, do-it-yourself graphics, bookmarks and magnets but with a twist, in order to gather the customer's attention.

Let me share the example of a bootstrapped start-up in Madurai called VE CLEAN, which was into toilet cleaning services.[4] They had a target to get 100 new subscriptions within the next 30 days. So they ran a marketing campaign for a community in Madurai which said, 'When was the last time you cleaned your toilet?' They undertook the challenge of cleaning all toilets of the 400 odd houses in the community within the next 24 hours and planned it accordingly. They did a very good job of it. They not only earned goodwill and brand visibility but also 84 subscriptions within a single day. And what was their cost? It was less than ₹10,000. So by adopting outlier marketing, your business stands to gain.

Collaborative Marketing

Collaborations are a great way to cross-promote and market each other to reach new customers. Instead of competing with rivals, think if there is a way you can market each other. This way of marketing is not only cost-effective but also effective as someone else is showcasing your service/product. As a member of the Professional Speakers Association, I have noticed this way of marketing. In this example of collaborative marketing, each member markets the other speaker as each speaker offers a different speaking niche; the members collaborate to promote and market each other. This is done in an informal manner. However, in associations such as BNI (Business Network International), I understand that it is done in a formal manner.

---

[4] Pravin Shekar, *Devil Does Care: More Bang, Less Bucks!* (Chennai: Notion Press, 2016).

Another example of collaborative marketing: Chennaigaga is a brand which sells unique Chennai T-shirts and souvenirs, which became the official partner of the Chennai Super Kings (CSK), selling exclusive CSK merchandise. CSK is a cricket team which participates in the Indian Premier League (IPL).

Watch Out for These Common Mistakes

The common mistakes that businesses commit regarding the cost-effective marketing strategies are as follows:

- Thinking that marketing means it involves huge spending.
- Not thinking out of the box for unique marketing ideas.
- Not setting a budget nor a limit on the marketing spend.
- Not focusing on the right target audience.
- Not leveraging on various digital means.

FINANCIAL THREATS IN MARKETING

A business can spend much money on marketing and yet there are chances that it is a failed attempt because the acceptance from the customer can never be predicted. Tata came out with the cheapest car Nano with the intention to make the car affordable for everyone. So the tagline they came up with was 'The cheapest car'; unfortunately, the word 'cheap' did not resonate well with many and thus the marketing of the Nano car went on to become a fiasco. So watch out and ensure the marketing spend is not wasted.

While incurring huge amounts on advertisement, your business needs to be extra prudent and cautious as it could backfire.

Another example is that of a particular advertisement of Tanishq jewellery.[5] One set of people were all praises for the advertisement, while a group of religious activists shunned it. Soon after releasing and after many appreciating the advertisement, Tanishq decided to remove the advertisement. The ones who had appreciated this advertisement did not like the fact that Tanishq had removed this advertisement because of religious sentimental issues. Thus, it received flak both ways apart from spending a huge amount on the advertisement.

However, there is another school of thought on this particular advertisement, which they claim is a planned move of Tanishq on the advertisement, for the sake of gaining branding and becoming a talking point.[6] According to this school, Tanishq has capitalized on the positive power of curated controversies and that the advertisement was orchestrated.

I am not getting into this debatable issue but only highlighting how marketing can also be played upon to suit your requirement. For you to do this, you need to take calculated risks to ensure that you get the required mileage from marketing and that it does not backfire.

Marketing can make or break and hence it requires a lot of thought before finalizing the way it wants to reach the customers. Some of the marketing campaigns such as Ariel's 'Share the load' (stating that doing the

---

[5] https://www.youtube.com/watch?v=LMOHY4naVYA
[6] https://www.youtube.com/watch?v=cjWixwq6_1A&feature=youtu.be

laundry was gender neutral), Vodafone's ZooZoos, Fevikwik's 'Todo nahi jodo' (when translated, it means not to break but to join) and Amul butter (which relies on cartoons based on the current happenings) are excellent examples of successful marketing campaigns.

What is the message you are sending to your market with your marketing initiatives?

Tangible versus Intangible Returns

The returns from a marketing campaign can be tangible or intangible. It is tangible when it helps in converting to sales and intangible could be in brand positioning, brand building and having a high recall value in the minds of the customer. The brand name becomes synonymous with the product; for example, in India, instead of the term 'photocopying', many people just say, 'Xerox copy'. While branding your business, you need to understand the finer details, for instance, the colours that you choose for your business brands have significance—blue denotes trust, yellow depicts warmth, green for growth, etc. Similarly, if your business wants celebrities for endorsements, they come at a premium. You must be sure of recovering not only the cost of the celebrity and the advertisement but also much more from the financial perspective.

What sort of intangible benefits are you seeking from your marketing campaign?

Business competitors also get into an advertising war to capture not only a larger market share but also the mind-share of the customer so that their brand has the top recall value when the customer thinks of the product. Pepsi and Coke have advertising wars, trying to be on top of each other, and marketing plays a very important role for them.

For your business to have a successful marketing strategy, it would be good to study the customer needs, behaviours, patterns, pricing expectations, etc. Having a market study done and/or undertaking a market research could help. The amount incurred in these market studies/ research and the marketing should get reflected in the sales for these efforts to become successful. However, one should not expect an overnight success and should be willing to give it some time to see the full results.

Few businesses such as Amway, Oriflame and Tupperware use multi-level marketing (MLM) or network marketing or direct marketing approaches, thus keeping their marketing costs at a minimum. They incur commissions on every sale made, instead of marketing costs. However, a word of caution is that MLM is considered illegal in some countries.

> iLearning was a global network marketing company which had to shut shop suddenly. Prasanna Venkatesh C. B., who was a direct selling representative, says that despite having big names such as Brian Tracy, Bob Proctor, Jim Cathcart and many more to build an online global learning company, it failed because the pricing model was not unique for each geography, and there was no sufficient value for money. If you are considering network marketing, take your pick wisely.

Watch Out for These Common Mistakes

The common mistakes that businesses commit regarding the financial aspects of marketing are as follows:

- Incurring huge spend on marketing without having clarity on the intended audience.

- Spending on marketing but not thinking from the customer's perspective.
- Treading on taboo, sentimental or emotional aspects of the customer in an incorrect manner, leading to failure of the marketing campaign.
- Not tracking nor measuring the returns from the marketing spend.
- Not consciously working on building the brand of the business.

ROI ON MARKETING

An essential way to measure and ensure that marketing is successful is the ROI. Whatever the amount incurred on marketing should ideally get translated into multiple times as revenue and thereby enable the business to grow.

Are Your Marketing Efforts Worthwhile?

There are instances when marketing is done incorrectly; there are no conversions and hence the entire amount spent is not fruitful. This is especially common in digital marketing. While it seems simple, businesses that place the advertisements on Google, Facebook, Instagram, etc., have not had any leads generated from it. This could be because of multiple reasons such as not defining the correct target audience, the advertisement does not convey the right message or does not resonate with the customer, cluttered advertisement and USP or outcomes not clearly highlighted. So while marketing, the basic hygiene factors must be ensured so that the returns through marketing are high, and it facilitates business growth.

Pradeep P. S., the founder of Farmers Fresh Zone, a bootstrapped start-up in Cochin, shares that as part of the expansion, they devised a marketing strategy to hire a senior marketing professional from a reputed company. They managed to achieve 40 per cent top-line growth. One reason for the growth was the introduction of cashback offers to customers. However, soon they realized that although the revenue increased, the cashback was eating into their margins and affecting their cash flow. Their marketing costs rose multiple times, resulting in reduction in margins despite the revenue growth. Upon discovering this financial impact on their cash flow and margins, Farmers Fresh Zone immediately withdrew cashback and strategized to add better value to customers.

In contrast to the above is the marketing strategy of another start-up called The Earth Lovers, which is into a range of eco-friendly self-care products and is based in Ariyalur district in Tamil Nadu. The founder Asvene Sekar says that in order to boost their sales, they gave an attractive offer to their customers which was 'Buy one, get to try four samples for free'. This resulted in the number of customers as well as the sales to double. My next question to Asvene was on the margin impact because of this offer, and I was surprised to note that the margin also improved by 5 per cent. The secret behind this increase was Asvene's marketing strategy. She decided not to spend on advertising and instead whatever amount they used to spend earlier on advertising was now channelized in giving discounts to the customers. She adds that this has also resulted in creating goodwill, and her customers are referring more customers in turn.

So you need to carefully design winning marketing strategies, which are specific to your business.

Market Potential

While designing the marketing plan, it is essential to take into account the market potential. For instance, if you are in the business of construction, the market offers the potential to construct in every city, every town and every village. Where is it that you want to focus? What is your construction niche? By defining this and focusing correctly, you can save your energy and costs by working on your specialization and to the right target customer. So plan your marketing accordingly.

How are you ensuring that these hygiene factors are in order for your business?

Some businesses prefer to outsource the function of marketing. It has its pros and cons, and you must be prudent to choose the best option for your business.

Advantages of outsourcing marketing for your business are as follows:

- A pool of experts and specialists are working for your business.
- You need not focus on this area as it is not your core.
- Not a recurring cost, as the agreement can be terminated as agreed upon.
- Unbiased views of an external person, who is reading your case with a fresh pair of eyes.
- The outsourced team is updated with the latest industry trends.
- Reduction of headcount from your team.
- You have the flexibility of working with different agencies.

Disadvantages of outsourcing marketing for your business are as follows:

- Expensive as compared to having an in-house team.
- Dependence and relying on an external team.
- You are tied up with the same agency for the period of the contract.
- Possibility of sharing of your business secrets, operations, etc., with third parties.
- History and continuity of the marketing could be lost as it is outsourced.
- Chances of leaking information with your competitors.
- Getting the marketing know-how at a later date (especially if you want to move away from the outsourced agency) could be a challenge.

Ensure you make an informed decision on the outsourcing of marketing.

Marketing Funnel

To visualize and understand the process of converting your potential customers into real customers of your business is what a marketing funnel does. If the funnel is broken down into steps, this is how it would look like:

1. The mouth of the funnel is catering to all your potential customer leads through marketing campaigns, events, advertising, social media, etc.
2. The next step is to evoke interest through engagements, positioning, specific content, etc., to the interested leads.
3. The interested leads are further narrowed down with product information, case studies, free trials, etc., and this is the contribution stage.
4. Next is the intent where the lead is nurtured through product demos, answering specific queries, automated email campaigns, etc., to attract your customer further.
5. The last but one stage is the stage where the lead is evaluating and deciding where to buy your product or

service from, and you need to prove and reiterate why yours is the best option for them.

6. The last stage is where the lead becomes your customer, and the sales transaction is completed and you have your customer!

During each stage of the marketing funnel, you need to carefully evaluate and understand the financial implication. If it is not being fruitful or not generating enough, you should ensure that no further amount is spent or moderate the money outflow carefully so that it maximizes your returns from marketing.

Cost of Customer Acquisition

The cost of customer acquisition is the cost of converting and getting a lead to buy your product or service. And this cost is related to the life time value of the customer. A shrewd business person will have a constant watch on this financial metric and ensure that this number is kept at a minimum as this has a significant positive impact on profits. Lower the cost, higher the profit. So if you have incurred 1,000 bucks on marketing and acquired 100 customers, your cost of customer acquisition is 10 bucks per customer. Calculate the past and the current cost of customer acquisition. Set limits for the cost of customer acquisition under different scenarios.

Impact of Guerrilla Marketing

Some businesses adopt this marketing route to promote a particular brand or service and use an advertisement strategy of guerrilla marketing. Here, they use a surprise element or unconventional interactions for promotions. This is mainly for publicity and creating brand value. This strategy is adopted for a high recall value and a stickiness quotient of the brand. It could be in the form of a flash mob, stencil graffiti, creative and unique videos, etc. An example of this is the Volkswagen advertisement: Speed up your life - Take the slide.

So while this is a good marketing strategy, you need to have an eye on the costs as well and ensure that the sales generated out of this are multiple times higher than the cost incurred.

A word of caution: If you decide to be extra creative with your guerrilla marketing ideas to the other extreme, watch out.

> Two guys ran onto the field in a rugby match between New Zealand and Austria wearing nothing but the logo of Vodafone painted on their bodies.[7] It received fierce public outrage that the CEO had to apologize and cough up an amount towards charity. On one side, yes you could say that it was inappropriate, but well on the other side you could argue that it was effective as well! No wonder it is said that marketing is a grey area.

Should you wish to track your marketing progress, here is a template which you can customize as per your requirements.

Parameters to Track	Amount (₹)	Tangible Benefit (Sales/Leads Generated, ROI, etc.)	Intangible Benefit (Reach/Leads/Branding/Followers, etc.)
Content marketing			
– Vlog			
– Blog			

---

[7] http://www.creativeguerrillamarketing.com/guerrilla-marketing/18-of-the-most-memorable-guerrilla-marketing-campaigns/

Parameters to Track	Amount (₹)	Tangible Benefit (Sales/Leads Generated, ROI, etc.)	Intangible Benefit (Reach/Leads/ Branding/Followers, etc.)
– Social media post			
Search engine optimization			
Digital marketing			
– Facebook			
– Instagram			
– LinkedIn			
Traditional advertising			
– Television			
– Radio			
– Newspaper			
– Hoarding			
– Posters			
Website			

Set aside the required percentage of sales towards your future marketing spend, which will enable you to grow your business further.

Watch Out for These Common Mistakes

The common mistakes that businesses commit regarding the ROI of marketing are as follows:

- Not tracking the ROI through marketing periodically.

- Not developing strategies to improve the ROI on marketing.
- Not having the required clarity on whether to outsource the function of marketing or not, and deciding on outsourcing without clearly defining the expected outcome.
- Not clearly articulating the action to be taken by the potential customer after watching the advertisement/promotion/website (like buy now, book this product, get in touch to know more, etc.).
- Not working enough to create and build a brand.
- Not performing a periodic review and tweaking the campaign according to the responses evoked from the leads.
- Not considering the intangible benefits of brand building.

Build Your Marketing Action Plan

Marketing is essential, especially if you are keen to grow your customer base. Think through the steps you can take to improve your top line through marketing. Take a call on when you want to be bullish or bearish in marketing. Vary it as per the customer demands and seasonal fluctuations (if any). Instead of going overboard with your marketing spend, you can moderate and set limits so that you can control it better.

Rank your current level under each line as Low or Average or Good or Great. Arrive at the desired level and the actions that will get you to the desired level. Measure the financial impact of the action on the top line or bottom line or cash flow. State the non-financial impact of the action. If a topic is not applicable for your business, skip that and move on to the next. To prioritize

S. No.	Topic	Current Level	Proposed Level	Actions To Be Taken	Financial Impact (on Top Line/ Bottom Line/ Cash Flow)	Non-financial Impact (on Branding, Visibility, Recall Value by Customer, etc.)
1	Ways to grow business through referral marketing					
2	Evaluate the digital marketing strategies					
3	Frugal ways to grow your business's top line					
4	Outlier marketing ways to grow the profitability					
5	Gauge your options to collaborate					
6	Enhance the tangible outcome of the marketing campaign					
7	Enhance the intangible outcome of the marketing campaign					
8	Check the hygiene factors of your marketing strategy					

(Continued)

(Continued)

S. No.	Topic	Current Level	Proposed Level	Actions To Be Taken	Financial Impact (on Top Line/ Bottom Line/ Cash Flow)	Non-financial Impact (on Branding, Visibility, Recall Value by Customer, etc.)
9	Assess the outsourcing options of marketing					
10	Build the marketing funnel of your business					
11	Outcome from challenging your current beliefs about your business					
12	Ways to decrease the cost of customer acquisition					
13	Assess if the marketing is directed to the right target audience					
14	Guerrilla marketing ways to increase sales					
15	Ensure there is a call to action (CTA) in your marketing initiative					

your action plan, segregate between 'must-have' and 'desirable' actions.

Thoughts for Reflection/Action

- What is the marketing budget that you have set for your business?
- What are the various ways by which you can enhance your ROI on marketing?
- What is the story your marketing funnel is telling you?
- Make a list of the intangible benefits your business has acquired through the various marketing initiatives.
- What are the values your brand represents?
- How is the customer perceiving your brand?

LEADERS SPEAK

Marketing Is a Science, Practised as an Art
Interview of Mr Chella Pandyan, Chief Marketing Officer and Marketing Director, Kimberly-Clark India

BRANDING VERSUS ADVERTISING VERSUS MARKETING

Marketing is a larger umbrella, starting from identifying the need till fulfilment. Advertisement is creating not only brand awareness but also the desire to buy. Branding is meant to create a trademark which will be relatable by the buyer. It is also a promise of fulfilling expectations. Therefore, branding is a subset of advertising, and advertising is a subset of marketing. For financial growth, a business needs to leverage all of these.

Marketing also includes the component of innovation. For example, many years ago, chocolates were not sold in smaller towns and villages due to the lack of refrigeration facilities. When a marketer is faced with such issues, they have to be innovative with the product as well as overcome potential challenges. In this case, in order to cater to the specific market of smaller towns in India, Cadbury innovated with a format they marketed as Cadbury Dairy Milk Shots, which was chocolate covered with a thin sugar coating, which would keep the chocolate from melting as it went into non-refrigerated stores. Marketing can be seen as leveraging and understanding the needs, desires and psychology of people and creating solutions to address them. And by understanding this, through marketing, a business can boost its revenue.

TRADITIONAL ADVERTISING VERSUS DIGITAL ADVERTISING

Businesses could grapple with this dilemma. However, advertising is meant to create a positive response from the target audience. Therefore, the intention should be to choose the right medium(s) to reach the message to the intended recipient. So it narrows down to the fact where the intended recipient is present. Designing the advertising strategy of a business depends on where the audience for the product or service lies. For example, if the intended audience is in the rural segment, then advertising will have to take the traditional route of television, radio, etc. It is essential to choose the appropriate medium depending on the target.

After choosing the right medium, the important aspect to be examined is the point of receptivity. One needs to check if the audience are receptive to the communication and messaging. These days, people normally prefer to have byte-sized consumption. Therefore, the kind of information and amount of information play a key role along with the relevance of the advertising medium to the target intended consumer. Based on that, one should decide where to play, and then how to win is about choosing points of receptivity. As an example, for some categories, consumers are most receptive to recommendations from friends and family and such recommendations are much more powerful than an advertisement.

Digital is a powerful medium to grow the brand and the revenue and cannot be ignored especially if the intended audience are using that platform.

TARGET GROUPS

While marketing a product (or a service), having a clear definition of the target group of the intended audience makes it more specific. When the brand is large, there could be a challenge in narrowing down the target audience, as the consumers may be from a wide range. For example, one can argue that a product like chocolate can be meant for any age group and any class of society. However, the targeting needs to be sharp, disciplined and structured to communicate the right message for better results. To market to a certain target segment, the brand must understand their tastes and preference and communicate with them in a manner which would connect them with the brand and the chocolate. By not having the required clarity on the target audience, a brand loses the ability to communicate effectively with any group. Irrespective of a big or small brand, it is important to have a well-defined target audience for successful marketing to enable top-line growth.

BUILDING A MARKETING STRATEGY

A good marketing strategy is a disciplined set of processes in pursuit of business goals. It starts with the specific marketing tasks which are needed to achieve the business goals while being aware of whom it is meant for.

'Where to play' and 'how to win' are crucial aspects which need to be clearly defined. Strategies can be different for each segment, and a good understanding of the factors which play a role in decision-making will work well. A strategy is a process of identifying target recipients and understanding their needs and barriers to achieve the desired outcome. Thinking about 'How to win better' will drive the business ahead.

In marketing, the reach and frequency are important metrics to track. While ROI is a key metric, no one can be confident that the sale happened because of the advertisement or the marketing strategy. It could be because a friend referred or for any other reason the person was attracted to buy the product (or service). And therefore one can never be so sure.

In digital marketing, a key metric is the CTR (click-through rate) and thereafter the conversions as customers. The marketing funnel is different for different mediums, and all of them need to be tracked. Therefore, reach, frequency, conversions, repeat and loyalty are various indicators that would reveal the success of marketing. The sub-metrics within the marketing funnel are also parameters which need to be tracked for a greater ROI.

BRANDING

Great brands are built by a combination of tangible and intangible benefits through marketing initiatives. By doing so, the brand equity (which is a sum total of the intangibles which a consumer associates with a brand) enhances. And brands are built by beliefs, insights and inspiration, which may not be completely measured by ROI. Human psychology is such that in the majority of the cases, the decision comes first and then the rationalization. Hence, measuring the intangibles is the holy grail of marketing. Attention is required to manage and grow a brand.

MARKETING SPEND

There are no hard and fast rules on the amount to be spent on marketing. Normally for an FMCG business, the spend on marketing is around 6–10 per cent of the turnover. The amount to be spent on marketing is subject to the task which needs to be accomplished. A new product requires more amount to be spent on marketing vis-à-vis an existing and well-established product or brand. It is therefore contextual and consumer task dependent. In order to arrive at ideal marketing spend, a business can break it down into the following:

- What is the business task which needs to be done to achieve the desired result?
- How to spend the amount in order to achieve the result?

- And based on the above answers, the marketing budget can be tweaked.
- If the amount is a constraint, one should think creatively to manage within the set amount.

For a small marketing budget to work well, there needs to be sharper focus on identification of the target audience as well as utilizing the marketing tools and means effectively with clarity in messaging. Content marketing is the best way of frugal marketing.

Some of the important financial metrics which one can measure and track from marketing spend include lifetime value, cost to reach customer, cost of retention, cost of acquisition, repeat ratios, recommendation ratios, online product/service ratings, conversion ratios, brand loyalty, brand journey, etc.

Without having a marketing funnel one cannot market a product. It is an abstraction of the users' behaviour. Price, reliability, style, etc., are the factors that play a role in decision-making. The focus can be on creating more numbers at the mouth of the funnel or increasing the number of conversions for the marketing initiative to become more successful. So every marketer should know his funnel. Marketing is a science because it is replicable and the principles are simple.

MARKETING MANAGEMENT

To manage marketing successfully, a good marketing team has to pay attention to the entire marketing funnel—from the understanding of consumer to consumer insights to product delivery. This will help in minimizing the marketing costs and enhancing revenue growth. A successful marketing initiative is when the brand is able to deliver what the consumer wants and creates a delight in the expectations. A mismatch between understanding and delivery is a fiasco, for instance, a good product but delivered to the wrong person. Similarly, flimsy or not thought-through problem definition is a failure. A humble and open-minded problem definition is important; otherwise, even if the marketing initiative succeeds, it does not become a replicable model as there is no clarity on what contributed to the success.

07

FINANCIAL MANAGEMENT WITH SUPPLIERS

CORE OF THE SUPPLY FUNCTION: SOURCING SUPPLIES WITHIN THE DEFINED SCOPE

Suppliers are important especially for manufacturing organizations as the business is dependent on the raw materials from the suppliers. However, even if you are in the services business, you will still rely on your vendors and suppliers for your business-related procurement. The supply relationship depends on the pricing, quality, timeliness, rapport and agreed terms and conditions for smooth transactions. So by effectively managing your suppliers, you can get the cost advantage for your business. And whatever cost is saved helps you grow your profits.

The purchase function aims to do the following:

- Acquire the goods or services at minimum cost
- Ensure smooth flow of operations
- Ensure timely delivery
- Utilize funds optimally
- Ensure good quality so as to serve the customer good quality

Your purchase could be direct or indirect. Direct purchases are the purchases which are directly related to the turnover of the business (like raw materials, etc.), and indirect purchases are those goods and services which are required for day-to-day operations and smooth running of the business. Your purchase should be at the right time at the right price from the right supplier.

Depending on your nature of business and your cash position, you can adopt any of the following types of purchases.

1. *Requirement based:* Purchases which happen as and when required and nothing is purchased in advance. This works well when there is precision in planning.

2. *Cyclical purchase:* When the purchases are based on periodic intervals and a pre-scheduled basis. When there is good visibility and discipline in the process, this method is effective.

3. *Market based:* This method of purchasing is resorted to take advantage of the price variations and earn some extra money in the process.

4. *Contract based:* This is like a blind date as the buyer does not know which items will be ordered but is like a binding agreement. It has the advantage of low price of materials with fluctuating costs.

Purchases should be made based on the study of market conditions and industry trends. Post the pandemic, with many businesses working from home (or working from anywhere), managing remote teams effectively is essential. As this could be the normal way of functioning of a business going forward, create a process flow for procurement approvals, empanel and empower your suppliers and vendors as well as redesign your purchase policies and procedures, keeping the future way of working in mind. You may also want to consider procurement digitization which makes it easier for your empanelled vendors as well. If you have other branches, you can consider centralizing all the purchases to take advantage of economies of scale.

If your business has a separate procurement or purchase division (or whoever is in charge of the purchases), that department needs to ensure the following:

- Best price
- Great quality
- Selecting the right vendor/supplier
- Obtaining necessary approvals
- Purchase digitization (in conjunction with the IT team)
- Build rapport and harmonious relationships with suppliers
- Settlement of complaints

The purchase function can be centralized or decentralized. Both have their advantages and disadvantages.

The advantages of centralized purchase include the following:

1. Volume discounts
2. Standardization of materials used and hence no variation because of the ingredients used
3. Efficiency in inventory management
4. Time reduction in terms of no duplication of efforts and therefore the people hours spent on researching the material, seeking comparative quotes, etc.

The disadvantages of centralized purchase are as follows:

1. Lack of flexibility in other locations
2. Extra spend on sending the materials to other locations
3. Lack of autonomy
4. Time lag in updating the purchase department

The advantages of decentralized purchase include the following:

1. Purchase as and when required based on consumption
2. No extra cost on transportation or warehousing
3. Right quantity of purchase
4. Replacement of defective materials is less time-consuming

The disadvantages of decentralized purchase are as follows:

1. Bulk discount options may not be possible
2. The staff may not have the requisite knowledge in purchasing
3. Lack of cooperation and coordination between the departments
4. Duplication of efforts in seeking quotes, understanding requirements, processing of payments, etc.

Building and nurturing a good network of suppliers and vendors contributes to the top-line growth. Here is some food for thought for you based on the following example.

According to Balasubramanian P. C., Managing Director of Matrix Business Services, about 25 years ago, their business disrupted the service delivery model in the business assurance services space by creating a huge network of chartered accountants' firms to handle tasks at their respective locations throughout the country. This speeded up the execution, reduced their cost of delivery, benefited their clients and the business surged by 50 per cent every year for the first four years. A new sustainable and scalable model was thus created through a collaborative network. This boosted business opportunities and was still very competitive on the pricing front. This model enabled inclusive growth and is still live and kicking.

Figure 7.1. Profit Hack Wheel of the Supply Function

For your business to pivot on supplies and procurement from the cost angle, the following points can be explored further:

1. What is the impact of the purchases on cash flow?
2. How to ensure adherence to legal aspects while working with different suppliers?

3. How to make cost-effective purchases?
4. How to manage suppliers efficiently?

The answers to the above questions are collated together and are represented as the profit hack wheel of the supplier function in Figure 7.1.

CASH FLOW IMPACT

While any purchase or supplies implies money going out, how can your business make the best out of it? Prima facie, you can play around with the credit period, the time of purchasing or sometimes on volumes and cash. Here are some more pointers.

If your business is cash-rich, you can consider paying without a credit period and seek a discount for not using the credit period. This extra discount can contribute to the bottom line of the business.

However, if your business is hard-pressed for cash, negotiate on the maximum possible credit period and ensure you are able to pay it within the time frame. If your business is dealing with an MSME vendor (or if your business is an MSME vendor), remember that in India, these vendors need to be paid within 45 days; otherwise, interest starts to accrue and they can subsequently be liable for legal action.

Here is an instance.

A large European MNC, which had its factory in India, did not want the contract staff as part of their payroll. Hence, they had outsourced its payroll activity of the contract staff to a vendor, who was an MSME vendor. Each month, the invoice value was substantial as it involved the total amount of the payroll of the contract staff plus the charges of the vendor. The vendor would get the invoice value paid only after 60 days as part of the payment cycle of the MNC. Due to the changes at the global headquarters, the organization decided to stop outsourcing the payroll of the contract staff. There were some old, disputed invoices of the vendor which were pending for over a few months. The invoices were settled subsequently after few months. However, when the MSME vendor got to know about the credit period for settling the invoices of the MSME vendors, he realized that the interest due to his business from the disputed invoice was a very large amount for his business. He wanted to recover this amount. He had three options: to amicably get it resolved, write about this legal non-compliance to the headquarters in Europe or take the legal option. Luckily, after some rounds of discussion with the officials, he recovered this amount.

Another way to carefully manage your cash is through just-in-time (JIT) purchase or planned purchase. The orders placed with the supplier are placed after careful planning, depending on the production quantity. This has two advantages:

- Your working capital is not stuck in raw materials
- You do not have to stock the materials

For instance, a printing company used to buy large quantities of paper and stock it for its printing requirements. Due to stocking the large quantities of paper, they used to incur warehousing charges. But once they started planning their printing process meticulously, they started purchasing the right quantity required and benefited from reduced warehousing charges as well as better working capital management.

A word of caution: By resorting to JIT, you need to be careful and ensure that your suppliers are able to regularly supply as per your needs and that your business does not face any shortages.

Cash Budget

You can also prepare your cash flow budget as this will give you good visibility and help you plan better to make the right financial decision. During some months, the cash flow could be negative or have a low positive balance, and if you are planning a huge cash out (e.g., procuring equipment) during those months, it would help you plan better the months in which you have a good cash position and help you take decisions accordingly. Similarly, many businesses pay a bonus to the staff during the big Indian festival of Diwali. As Diwali can be either in October or in November, you can plan your cash flow better and make necessary adjustments to your cash outflow. Below is a sample cash flow budget which tracks the movement of money in and money out.[1]

Note that the cash budget needs to be prepared based on the movement of cash; that is, it is based on the cash movement of money in and money out. Slot the amounts in respective months you think money will be required to be paid. Like you notice in Table 7.1, the cash balance is negative during the months of April and May. Therefore, if you were planning to buy expensive equipment, your decision to purchase the fixed asset needs to be postponed from April to June or needs to be paid in instalments. Alternatively, you need to look for other sources to pay it.

Thus, preparing the cash flow budget gives you visibility to plan your cash.

---

[1] Sangeeta Shankaran Sumesh, *What the Finance: Easy-to-learn Finance Practices for Entrepreneurs Who Want to Achieve High Performance* (Chennai: Notion Press, 2019).

Particulars	Months					
	Jan	Feb	Mar	Apr	May	Jun
Opening balance	**50,000**	**259,000**	**139,000**	**38,000**	**–37,000**	**–28,000**
Receipts						
Cash sales	10,000	7,000	5,000	8,000	5,000	6,000
Receivables from Customer A	150,000	–	100,000	200,000	90,000	150,000
Receivables from Customer B	60,000	50,000	30,000	20,000	50,000	80,000
Receivables from Customer C	250,000	75,000	125,000	350,000	180,000	200,000
Interest earned	5,000	12,000	7,000	2,000	–	–
Scrap sale	–	–	–	10,000	–	–
Total cash available	**525,000**	**403,000**	**406,000**	**628,000**	**288,000**	**408,000**
Payments						
Salaries	200,000	200,000	200,000	200,000	200,000	200,000
Bonus	–	–	–	200,000	–	–
Rent	30,000	30,000	30,000	30,000	30,000	30,000
Electricity	5,000	5,000	5,000	5,000	5,000	5,000

(Continued)

(Continued)

Particulars	Months					
	Jan	Feb	Mar	Apr	May	Jun
Opening balance	**50,000**	**259,000**	**139,000**	**38,000**	**–37,000**	**–28,000**
Insurance	–	–	75,000	–	–	–
Office supplies	7,000	7,000	7,000	7,000	7,000	7,000
Repairs and maintenance	2,000	2,000	5,000	2,000	2,000	5,000
Travel	4,000	5,000	4,000	5,000	4,000	5,000
Connectivity costs	3,000	3,000	3,000	3,000	3,000	3,000
Purchase of fixed asset	–	–	–	200,000	–	–
Professional fees	10,000	10,000	10,000	10,000	10,000	10,000
Audit fees	–	–	–	–	50,000	–
Income tax payments	–	–	25,000	–	–	25,000
Miscellaneous	5,000	2,000	4,000	3,000	5,000	2,000
Total cash required	**266,000**	**264,000**	**368,000**	**665,000**	**316,000**	**292,000**
Closing balance	**259,000**	**139,000**	**38,000**	**–37,000**	**–28,000**	**116,000**

Table 7.1. Cash Flow Projection of ABC Enterprises for Six-month Period Ending June 20XX (in ₹)

Watch Out for These Common Mistakes

The common mistakes that businesses commit regarding the cash aspects of purchasing are as follows:

- Not planning the production in relation with the procurement.
- Failure to prepare a cash forecast or a cash budget.
- Not anticipating purchase requirements upfront.
- Blindly deciding on big purchases without knowing the exact cash position.
- Not taking into account the liquidity impact from the purchase routine.
- Not considering the open purchase orders issued while making financial decisions.

LEGAL ASPECTS OF SUPPLIES

A purchase is a transaction with a supplier who is bound by legal terms and conditions which are stated in the purchase order. However, there are times when you need to be extra cautious and take necessary precautions with regard to your business operations and trade secrets as vendors and suppliers may also sometimes be privy to your trade secrets. You need to know how to safeguard your business-related activities.

> The octogenarian Dr Nalli Kuppusami Chetty of Nalli Silks recalls an incident during my interview with him about an incident with his master weaver. A particular customer of Nalli Silks had placed an order with the special order division of the shop as she had created a specific design with an unusual combination and wanted the silk sari

woven by Nalli Silks. The design was given to the master weaver who was based in Kanchipuram to create the particular sari. He had asked for two months' time to weave the sari. After about a month, the customer was astonished to find a sari as per her colour combination and design specifications with another popular competing silk sari store. She immediately purchased it and took it to Nalli Silks saying that she got it without having to place an order. Nalli Silks immediately contacted the supplier as they were astonished at how this was possible. The master weaver went to the specific weaver's house to check how the design specifications were leaked. The master weaver discovered that the younger brother of the weaver happened to be the master weaver of the competing silk store and the brothers were neighbours and secrecy could not be maintained. So from a business standpoint of working with vendors and suppliers, you need to be careful to ensure that all possibilities of leakages are plugged and you do not incur any loss.

From a legal standpoint, it is always good to enter into a non-disclosure agreement (NDA) to legally safeguard business interests. However, there is no guarantee that the business secrets will remain guarded despite having the NDA in place. But should there be a legal dispute, an NDA could prove to be useful. Further, the vendor will also be cautious in not revealing information about your business.

While selecting your large suppliers, it is always good to perform due diligence and check their background so that you know the soundness of the vendor and your business is not in jeopardy or impacted by any of their shortcomings. You can have a specific supplier selection process with basic criteria set to narrow down the kind of suppliers you would like to work with. It would also be a healthy practice to gather necessary information about your vendor like their profile, PAN, GST registration, etc. Having the required documentation will come in handy.

Quality of Supplies Impacts Output

Clear specifications of the supplies need to be mentioned in the purchase order and also communicated exactly to the supplier. Further, you have to verify that the supplies match the specifications you want. Remember that the quality of your supplies is important as the reputation of your business is at stake. Quoting the example of Nalli Silks again, which was established in 1928, even now the Managing Partner Dr Nalli claims that he examines the woven silk sarees to check whether or not these meet their quality requirements. From a legal perspective, ensure that your contract with the supplier clearly and appropriately specifies the replacement policy, money back scheme, time taken to supply, etc., so that there is no ambiguity in case of any dispute at a later date.

Watch Out for These Common Mistakes

The common mistakes that businesses commit regarding the legal aspects of purchasing are as follows:

- Failing to enter into written contracts or agreements.
- Not having the habit of entering into an NDA.
- Not collecting sufficient information about the suppliers.
- Not evaluating legal implications.
- Not safeguarding business secrets from the vendors and suppliers.

COST-EFFECTIVE PURCHASES

Your purchase implies that money is going out. However, by ensuring a little bit of prudence and effective internal controls, there are good chances that your purchases can become cost-effective. Here are some suggestions on how you can deal with all your purchases.

Negotiate for Favourable Deals

Whenever and wherever possible, negotiate for better prices or better payment terms or better deals or any other additional benefit which may be possible. Many times I have noticed that some people do not like to negotiate (for fear of rejection or due to pride or any other reason) or forget about negotiation. If you are one such person who does not like to negotiate, the way to approach negotiation would be that there is nothing to lose. If it works in your favour, it's great; if not, there is nothing to sweat about. Negotiate not just on the purchase of products or assets but also when you seek services. Seek freebies if you can in any of your purchases.

Some areas of negotiations include the following:

- Suppliers and vendors (for discounts, better rates, terms and so on)
- Customers (encouraging bulk orders, quicker payment terms and so on)
- Investors (valuation, equity stake, rate of interest and so on)
- Bankers (for better credit facilities, lesser charges, better rate of interest and so on)
- Auditors (for lesser fees or combine consultation or seek their opinion as part of the audit fees)
- Other service providers (for better terms and conditions, scope for relaxing rules, any extras and so on)

In order to have effective negotiation skills, some of the complementary skills that you need to have are as follows:

- Good communication skills
- Excellent interpersonal skills
- Assertiveness
- Listening skills
- Decision-making skills
- Ethical business skills

As a rule, remember to negotiate in all your deals. Remember that through the combined effort of all your negotiations for your business-related purchases, significant cost reductions are possible.

Internal Controls on Purchases

Putting in place good internal control mechanisms especially for requisite approvals of your purchases can help. Also, a robust internal control mechanism will prevent frauds and thefts. Job rotation within the purchase department and the finance department can help minimize occurrences of frauds and thefts within your organization. Financial discipline in the form of a goods received note (GRN), which can track the quantity received, date and quality, can also act as a good audit trail.

Ensure that there is a budget for the purchase as well as necessary approvals before issuing the purchase order. Before issuing the invoice to process the payment, check for quality, damages, price, etc. Set this as a process as part of your internal controls so that you do not end up paying extra if there is no conformity to specifications.

Also, set up an efficient quality control process. Depending on the quantity, decide whether you prefer 100 per cent checking of the materials coming in or checking a sample. If you prefer the sample, what percentage of the materials would you like to be checked? Set these parameters upfront for your team to follow and comply with it. Further, check if the supplier is compliant with all the legal requirements as well as any specific compliances that may be warranted by your business or your industry.

Remember to mitigate the single source of supply for your business because if your supplier gets affected due to any reason, it impacts your business as well.

Comparative Quotes

The healthy habit of seeking quotations and comparing prices from other vendors helps you know that you are paying the right amount. Especially for large purchases, it would be ideal if you can seek three quotations to compare. This way you will also keep your vendors on their toes, and based on comparative quotes you can negotiate for the best deals. The comparison will also send a message to your vendor that they cannot mess with you as you are well aware of the current market rates and trends.

A word of caution: Quotes can sometimes be falsified or tweaked. Hence, you will have to apply prudence while evaluating the genuineness of the comparatives.

While comparing the prices, remember to also check for other related costs apart from the price such as transportation costs, delivery charges, import duty and applicable taxes. Remember to compare apples to apples. For example, a common loophole that many staff fall prey while booking hotel accommodation is on the pricing. The price per night quoted by hospitality agents or other similar websites could include taxes and breakfast, whereas for the same hotel the online rates in the hotel's website could be excluding taxes and breakfast. Thus, the staff are sometimes misguided and make the wrong choice of booking online from the hotel's website as prima facie they find the online price cheaper.

You could also check for ways and means to reduce purchasing costs by automating procurement workflow and thereby reducing both the time taken and paperwork involved. Another possible action could be end-to-end visibility of the inventory and tracing data for improving inventory management.

Hidden Costs

If your supplier does not deliver to you on time and it impacts your business operations, it could mean a potential loss of opportunity for you, which could result in loss of revenue. Apart from the loss of revenue, it could also mean that your resources are idle and thereby leading to idle cost or lack of utilization of resources. So be watchful of the opportunity cost and idle time cost and factor in them as well. Allocate specific purchases to exact cost centres or projects if it is associated with any particular project as it will come in handy while computing project profitability.

Watch Out for These Common Mistakes

The common mistakes that many businesses commit regarding purchases are as follows:

- Failing to obtain comparative quotes and blindly proceeding with one supplier.
- Not including other costs, taxes, etc., while comparing between price suppliers.

- Hesitating to negotiate for better deals.
- Lacking proper internal controls regarding purchase processes.
- Insufficient documentation for the purchase function (such as approvals, quotations, process flow and purchase order)
- Inefficient negotiation.

EFFICIENCY IN SUPPLIER MANAGEMENT

If you want to gain from your suppliers, some of the main parameters you need to consider for efficiency of your suppliers and vendors while you are evaluating them are as follows:

- *Price:* Competitive pricing, stability, accuracy, credit period given, etc.
- *Quality:* Matching specifications, durability, warranty, etc.
- *Time taken and delivery:* lead time, packaging, documentation, emergency delivery, etc.
- *Compliance:* With rules and regulations, laws, taxes, etc.
- *Service levels:* Time taken, efficiency, etc.
- *Behaviour:* – Reliability, trust factor, level of risk, etc.
- *After-sales support:* Timeliness, knowledge, availability of spares, technical support, emergency support, problem resolution, etc.
- Going concern of the supplier and dependability factor

You can also customize the supplier scorecard based on your requirements as per the following template:

Supplier Evaluation Scorecard (1: Least; 10: Highest)			
	Supplier A (score out of 10)	Supplier B (score out of 10)	Supplier C (score out of 10)
Price			
Quality			

Supplier Evaluation Scorecard (1: Least; 10: Highest)			
	Supplier A (score out of 10)	Supplier B (score out of 10)	Supplier C (score out of 10)
Delivery			
Time taken			
Compliance			
Behaviour			
Service levels			
After-sales support			
Going concern issues			
Total score			

Set your criteria while evaluating your vendors and rank them if required. For example, the ratings could be: extremely positive, positive, promising, neutral, negative, extremely negative, etc. The purchases your business makes need to be planned, tracked and recorded accordingly.

Your business may be dealing with a large number of suppliers. For you to get the most from your suppliers, it will be good to evaluate the performance of each supplier as it is a critical aspect of supplier management. Here are some steps that can assist you with it:

- Define the KPIs for your suppliers with product supply areas along with the appropriated weighted means for each of the KPIs.

- Further facilitate comparisons between the suppliers, identify the gaps in performance and rank your preferred suppliers.

- Provide feedback to suppliers to achieve desired levels of performance.

- Evaluate the supplier risk aspect both from a continuity and going concern aspect of your supplier and ensuring that your business secrets will remain intact with them.

- Examine the supplier behaviour for issues such as instances of fraud, non-compliance with labour laws and discrimination. These could impact your supply or your reputation. So be watchful.

- Watch out for your suppliers' supplier (or vendor's vendor) as that could also have an impact on your business.

Here is an example illustrating the last point in the above list.

An MNC had outsourced its housekeeping function to a large housekeeping agency. The agency in turn had outsourced the function to a smaller local agency. The housekeeping staff were on the roles of the smaller agency. Unfortunately, the smaller agency was having some cash issues and was not managed well from a finance perspective. Due to the poor financial management, the smaller agency was paying delayed salaries for the housekeeping staff. While most months the delay was anything between a week and 10 days, it came to light that the smaller agency was not remitting the PF amount and the ESI to the relevant authorities. Despite warnings, the large housekeeping agency failed to take necessary action of replacing the small vendor and as a result lost the contract with the MNC.

Thus, your supplier's supplier (or vendor's vendor) could also play role in managing the efficiency of your supplier.

Watch Out for These Common Mistakes

The common mistakes that businesses commit regarding supplier management are as follows:

- Not having a process in place for vendor evaluation.
- Not taking into account the compliance status of the supplier or vendor which could result in potential legal exposure.
- Relying too much on a single supplier. Should anything untoward happen to the supplier, the business operations are affected.
- Not checking the impact arising from the suppliers' supplier.
- Not clearly defining the KPIs for supplier management.
- Not having a clear plan on the logistics of the supplies as well as not having a risk mitigation plan.

Build Your Supplier Action Plan

You need to get a constant supply of materials and other essentials from all your suppliers, service providers and vendors for your business to be functioning efficiently.

Rank your current level under each line as Low or Average or Good or Great. Arrive at the desired level and the actions that will get you to the desired level. Measure the financial impact of the action on the top line or bottom line or cash flow. State the non-financial impact of the action. If a topic is not applicable for your business, skip that and move on to the next. To prioritize your action plan, segregate between 'must-have' and 'desirable' actions.

S. No.	Topic	Current Level	Proposed Level	Actions To Be Taken	Financial Impact (on Top Line/Bottom Line/Cash Flow)	Non-financial Impact (on Supplier Rapport, Documentation, etc.)
1	Evaluate pros and cons of JIT purchase for your business					
2	Prepare your cash budget for the next 12 months					
3	Prepare a list of all your suppliers and vendors with whom an NDA does not exist					
4	Devise a negotiation strategy for effective purchasing					
5	List all the vendors, service providers and suppliers with whom negotiations need to be done					
6	Define internal control mechanisms on the purchasing process					
7	Document the process of seeking comparative quotes					

8	Decisions based on supplier evaluation scorecard					
9	Define the KPI of your suppliers					
10	State ways by which you build rapport with your suppliers					
11	Prepare age-analysis of your suppliers to plan your cash outflow					
12	Prepare the risk mitigation strategy with your suppliers					
13	Assess the pros and cons of centralized versus decentralized purchasing for your business					
14	Make a list of your MSME vendors and ensure their payments are in line with the legal requirements					
15	Regularize the quality of output					

Thoughts for Reflection/Action

- Prepare the cash budget for the next one year and perform variance analysis of the cash outflow.
- What steps do you have in place for your business to reduce supplier risk?
- What internal controls do you have in place for all procurements in your organization?
- What are the negotiation tactics in place during the time of purchase?
- What is the process in place for evaluating your suppliers and vendors?

LEADERS SPEAK

Success with Suppliers
Interview of Mr Harish Lakshman, Vice Chairman, Rane Group

NEGOTIATION STRATEGY

Negotiation with suppliers can be adopted subject to whether technology is involved or certain trade secrets or a specific know-how is required. In our organization, we follow any of these ways to get the most cost benefit from our procurement.

1. Zero-based costing, wherein the buyer arrives at the price of a product with the help of in-house experts

or consultants. This price is then assessed against the comparative bids obtained and the gap is measured.

2. Reverse bidding or e-bidding, wherein suppliers who meet the specified quality requirements are invited online for a live bid to offer their best rates for the stated requirements. This real-time and transparent approach is adopted for certain non-critical components.

QUALITY CHECK

Robust systems are to be followed by the supplier as well as the customer, which are key to ensure that the quality of supplies is on par with the specifications. Before onboarding the vendors, there needs to be an onsite audit with detailed checklists and complete scrutiny of their process. For instance, at Rane, we have two exclusive departments which check for quality: supplier technical assistance (STA) and supplier quality assurance (SQA). The STA team checks if the supplier can deliver good quality consistently and the team performs repeat audits with rigorous checks. The SQA team validates that the supplies received are of good quality for use. Both these departments together minimize the probability of poor quality to a very large extent, saving not only reputation but costs as well.

TIMELINESS

In order to ensure that the suppliers are capable of delivering within the specified time, the STA department validates the suppliers' production capacity so that the end-customer delivery is not impacted. There are also possible external challenges like transport strike. To mitigate such risks, we use vendor-managed inventory (VMI), wherein the inventory required for two days of production is stocked in a warehouse near our factory so that we do not experience supply delays. This ensures that there is no stoppage of production and no unnecessary costs are incurred.

SUPPLIER RISK MANAGEMENT

Our suppliers are categorized as A, B and C, where category A represents highly critical and high-value supplies, B is moderate and C is for supplies that are not critical, low value and easily available. We prefer to deal with more than one supplier for a particular component so that the risk is spread across. If the component is unique in nature, then we opt for a single source, but it is usually for a medium term after which we get alternative suppliers to minimize the risk.

To mitigate the risks of trade secrets, exclusive product design, etc., it is always safe to ensure proper legal documentation such as NDA and contracts. This ensures that there is no information leakage. Apart from the legal aspect, trust also plays a crucial role. Once the trust is betrayed, there is no scope for future business apart from reputation loss in the industry.

Disputes with suppliers could arise due to quality, warranty, timeliness, etc., and need to be negotiated before arriving at an amicable solution. The negotiation is also leveraged upon future business prospects. While the legal route is an option, it is rare and resorted to only when there is no future with that particular supplier. Supplier risk management enables better control of costs.

REDUCTION IN PROCESS TIME

To reduce the supplier process time taken, early engagement and concurrent engineering are very important. When vendors are involved right from the beginning, even before a design is finalized, the vendors are aware of the thought process and they can start engineering based on these inputs. Thereby, majority of the design is ready and the remainder can be tweaked at a later date. This way, the given timelines are met. At Rane, we follow advanced product quality planning (APQP), which is a comprehensive system-based checklist, which also helps to shorten the time taken for product development and ensures first time right. This approach saves time, and time is money.

WASTAGES

The best way to minimize wastages is by planning quantities and related requirements. However, in cases where wastages cannot be avoided, it is best to factor these into the cost so that the business is not affected by it. Non-moving stock can also be minimized by planning and ultimately to be disposed and sold as scrap.

WORKING CAPITAL MANAGEMENT

JIT is a good way to manage inventory requirements as it also aids in better working capital management. Bill discounting and factoring assist in supplier payment cycle and help in realizing payments on time. At Rane, we review the payment cycle regularly and ensure that the suppliers are paid on time. When the supplier gets paid on time, it also helps the suppliers' supplier getting paid on time, thus ensuring that the cycle is smooth.

PRICE FLUCTUATIONS

In order to handle supplier price fluctuations, a healthy way to proceed is to opt for indexation where the prices are adjusted for in the subsequent quarter, failing which the entire onus is on either the supplier or the customer. For forex fluctuations, hedging or forward contracts could be useful.

OPERATIONAL EFFICIENCY

Efficiency in operations is of prime importance as that could be a key driving factor for profits. At Rane, we follow total quality management (TQM) systems for the right quality at the lowest cost within the shortest lead time and minimal wastage. We ensure detailed reviews through elaborate daily routine management practices. Every day, we analyse what went well and what did not. Identifying and closely managing all the variables which impact operations can ensure success for a business. For an MSME to be successful, it has to ensure that there are proper systems in place, which will enable long-term sustainability of the business.

<u>0</u>8

FINANCIAL WATCH WITH INFORMATION TECHNOLOGY

CORE OF THE IT FUNCTION: INFRASTRUCTURE THAT CREATES IMPACT FOR INCREMENTAL GROWTH

Companies all over the world are relying on emerging technology to help drive innovation, strategy and growth and create a competitive advantage. Technology has become a crucial part of most businesses. It is almost indispensable. Without technology in business, many businesses cannot think of surviving. Can a business function efficiently without the use of a telephone, computer or the internet? We have all become so dependent on technology. Technology in business continues to evolve and changes the way business is being done.

Leveraging IT can be a big boon for your business. IT enables speed, efficiency and accuracy. Having a strong IT team or a good outsourced IT partner can help your business in terms of automation and enhancing productivity levels. Thus, with technology, you can create increased financial value for your business and enhance the ability to evolve at a faster rate with existing or lesser resources.

With the onset of smart devices and gadgets, customer behaviour and preferences have changed over the years. And the pandemic has pushed all businesses to move towards digitization and use technology to grow their business. School and college education has moved to online classes. Even exams are happening online. Not only traditional education but fitness classes, cookery classes, book launches, exhibitions, weddings, etc., have also become virtual. With the use of the internet becoming more prevalent even in smaller towns and villages, using technology to grow your business has become a must. Location is no longer a major constraint.

The revenues of many businesses from e-commerce platforms have grown significantly as they have an efficient IT team driving the digital and tech aspects of the business. Having a website and good presence on social media platforms, enabling online sales, etc., have now become necessities and not a luxury like it was considered many years ago.

Not only have the banks enabled online banking facilities but apps such as Paytm and Google Pay have also become payment platforms. Even small shops on highways or in rural areas are utilizing these platforms to transact. Who would have guessed years ago that banks will face competition from newer industries?

Platforms such as Udemy, Teachable and Knorish have shrunk the world of education and made it more affordable as well. Businesses such as Swiggy, Ola and Oyo have built their business without owning assets but have completely leveraged technology to grow and diversify. Virtual meeting and video calling facilities through platforms such as Zoom, Airmeet, Google Meet and WebinarJam have brought the world closer. So with technology, not only the business barriers but physical barriers have also shrunk.

Businesses can improve both the performance and overall effectiveness of their products, systems and services through technology, because technology enables businesses to expand quickly and efficiently. Technology can impact operations, productivity, profitability and sustainability of an organization.

Technology aids communication—through electronic mails, live chat systems, etc.—which helps managers to stay in touch with their teams and oversee progress in work. Technology not only assists in communication at the workplace but also helps in connecting with clients.

Figure 8.1. Profit Hack Wheel of the IT Function

How can your business take advantage of IT for business growth? In this section, let us explore this option on the following factors:

1. How to enhance efficiencies through technology for business growth?
2. What steps can be taken to minimize the exposure related to financial threats arising from technology?
3. What are the risks involved in using technology?
4. How to control the associated IT costs involved?

The answers to the above questions are collated together and are represented as the profit hack wheel of the Information Technology function in Figure 8.1.

ENHANCING BUSINESS EFFICIENCIES

Management information systems (MIS) enable a business to track not only sales-related information but also expense classification and productivity of resources. The information that has been gathered can provide customized reports on every business function including competitor analysis. From the available data, identifying focus areas for growth, specific areas for improvement as well as untapped opportunities can be capitalized upon.

With the rapid enhancement of technology in the different walks of life, a business also needs to know how to utilize technology to its advantage. Some of the areas where your business can rope in technology, which could eventually help in financial growth, could be as follows:

- Improve CRM with software such as Zendesk, Zoho and Salesforce.
- Technology which enables the transfer of electronic files, speeding up workflow processes, etc., can save money by

saving space, stationery and printing costs. Examples of these are Dropbox, WeTransfer and SendTransfer.

- Through technology, the accounting procedures, accounting software and preparation of financial statements are made faster, and customized report generation is also possible. Commonly used accounting software are Tally, QuickBooks and Zoho Books.
- Inventory management, invoicing of customers and supplier management are all possible through technology, and different software are available for each activity.
- Processes that are repetitive can be digitized using technology.
- Technology can be applied to people management, and it improves the efficiency in recruitment, attrition management, screening and hiring potential candidates, performance tracking, etc.
- Another important role of technology in business is to provide security. Advancements in electronic security systems, biometric alarm systems and face recognition are helping in keeping businesses safe from hackers and thieves.

Management Information Systems

Effective utilization of MIS also involves detailed planning, designing the usage, organizing the data, coordinating with teams, operating and control of technology. So if you have the luxury, deploying a team to work on these aspects will be worthwhile. If not, you can also consider outsourcing this function. *The important aspect is how you are interpreting the data and what the corrective measures are that you are taking based on this towards business growth.*

By handling the management of information systems efficiently, your business can reduce its costs of operations, create new products, execute projects, penetrate new markets, improve customer service, streamline operations and benefit from a competitive advantage in the market. Both your business and your customers will get benefited, leading to business growth.

Artificial intelligence can be extremely useful to sift through large quantities of data in search of behavioural patterns and other insights. So is the case with data analytics software, which helps in analysing the required data, which would provide the necessary understanding to make the right business decisions.

Depending on whichever social media platform your business is active in, you can also utilize the social media analytics tools such as Facebook Business, LinkedIn Analytics, YouTube Analytics and Twitter Analytics and analyse and interpret the data to enable business growth. Further, devise ways and means to understand this data and brainstorm on how your business needs to progress to get to the next level. It would be good to brainstorm this with your entire senior management team to create a holistic path ahead for the business.

Technological Transformation for Business Growth

To design a technological transformation strategy for your business, you need to have a framework in place, which is a detailed plan that helps you make strategic updates to your systems and processes. The framework should also have comprehensive details on the following:

- *Vision:* What your business needs to accomplish through the technological transformation

- *Market study:* Understanding how technology will enable enhancement of your business and against competition
- *Customer experience:* Define the kind of customer experience you want to provide through the use of technology
- *Infrastructure requirements:* List down the new infrastructure needs or, if you can, modify the existing one to match the requirements.

For example, in the case of Netflix, it reinvented the way movies are being distributed. It is not just digital transformation but also leveraging on how technology can be used to completely reconstruct the existing business model.

Use of technology can help speed up your process. Quoting the example of Nalli Silks again, their designing process used to take three days earlier and now because of technology it happens within a day, as claimed by Dr Nalli. Similarly, using robotic process automation (RPA) and other latest developments, the process time can be significantly reduced, thereby enhancing the business efficiencies.

Some basics which you can use as a checklist while opting for the technological transformation which can enhance the efficiency of your business are as follows:

- Ease of use for customer, thereby enhancing customer experience
- No compromise on quality of the output
- Compute financial requirements of the proposed transformation and how it can be managed within your means
- Adherence to corporate governance, security features and foolproof security measures

- Maximize business performance through transformation
- Mitigation of associated risks arising out of the technological transformation
- Test the dependability of the technology
- Evaluate technology features from an internal controls' perspective
- Explore possibilities of utilizing automation, artificial intelligence, chatbots, etc.
- Check for recurring costs and slot them in your budget
- Handle employee/customer pushbacks against the transformation
- Ensure compliance with the legal aspects

Watch Out for These Common Mistakes

The common mistakes that businesses commit during technological transformation for business efficiencies are as follows:

- Not taking a holistic view of business requirements regarding the transformation.
- Not planning the financial requirements for transformation.
- Overlooking legal requirements.
- Not testing loopholes in the process which could give rise to security flaws.
- Not understanding or taking into consideration customer preferences.
- Not updating systems periodically.
- The IT team is sometimes not well equipped to handle the transformation.

EXPOSURE TO FINANCIAL THREATS

The security aspect is of utmost importance for the technology to be effective because any gaps in this can easily give way to hacking and other potential frauds, which could result in a huge business loss. Hence, careful planning and execution along with periodic updates are required. While protecting your information is extremely important, equally important is the recovery process in the case of a potential cyberattack. If attacked, it could be a quick destruction.

> Take the instance of the ransomware attack on the world's largest container shipping firm, Maersk. The attack had taken down the network, resulting in billions of dollars in damage and loss of revenue. Maersk had almost over 50,000 infected endpoints, thousands of applications and servers in over 600 sites across 130 countries which were hit with this attack. It caused a very serious business disruption. Recovering and rebuilding the network took many days for Maersk.[1]

So while protecting your network, the ultimate goal is to ensure that there is a data-recovery plan in place, in case of any such attacks. Define both preventive and recovery measures for your business and take the utmost precaution. Ensure that the data centre is well guarded.

Businesses also need to safeguard themselves from the attacks of the dark web. Necessary steps must be in place against all possible security threats. Businesses must also be wary of online transactions.

---

[1] https://www.zdnet.com/article/ransomware-the-key-lesson-maersk-learned-from-battling-the-notpetya-attack/

Here is an example.

> The CEO of a particular family-owned business was on a family vacation to an overseas location. During this time, the CFO received an email from the CEO, stating to urgently transfer an amount to a particular overseas bank account. The CFO called the CEO but the number was switched off. Not wanting to disturb the CEO while he was on a vacation with his family, the CFO decided to reply to the email to state that it will be transacted the next morning. Luckily, when the CFO hit the reply button to the email, he noticed something weird. The reply was going to a vague email address and not to the CEO's email address. Although the incoming mail had the exact mail address of the CEO with the correct name, etc., the outgoing mail proved that it seemed fishy. As soon as the CFO realized this, he alerted the IT team. The team traced the origins of the phishing mail to Spain, and it seemed obvious that it was not a genuine one.

Well-defined IT security systems should be in place to avoid such financial threats.

Watch Out for These Common Mistakes

The common mistakes that many businesses commit regarding technological safety are as follows:

- Not identifying blind spots in the technology system.
- Not performing a mock hack in order to plug the possibilities of hacking.
- Not designing proper preventive measures.

- Not ensuring the safety of the data centre.
- Not designing and implementing a suitable data-recovery plan.
- Not educating the teams on IT safety and security measures of the business.
- Not updating regularly the anti-virus, firewalls, etc.
- Exposure to potential threats from the internet, external devices, etc.

TECHNOLOGICAL RISKS AND THEIR MITIGATION

All aspects of the business are prone to risk, and technology is no exception. So while you cannot do away with risks, you can definitely take measures to minimize the exposure of your business to the risks involved. Remember that if your business has a website or if your employees are using a smartphone, there is an exposure to a possible cyberattack. These attacks are difficult to predict and understand. Therefore, it makes it important for you to figure out ways and means to mitigate the potential risks and save your business from potential losses.

As you can never claim to be 100 per cent cyber-secure, what you could opt for is being cyber-resilient. Being cyber-resilient is the ability to prepare and adapt to changing conditions so as to recover rapidly for possible disruptions. Cyber resilience starts at the top and should flow to the teams.

Risk Implications

The risk matrix in Figure 8.2 indicates the relationship between risk and digital transformation. When the rate of digital transformation is low, the time taken is longer and slower. When the transformation is high, the process is faster but one must be wary of the security concerns.

The risk to manage is lower when digital transformation is low and results in manual intervention, whereas when digital transformation is high it is experience-oriented. The risk is high when digital transformation is low, could cause control weakness and lapses but when digital transformation is high, it could provide rewards which are in proportion to the risk undertaken.

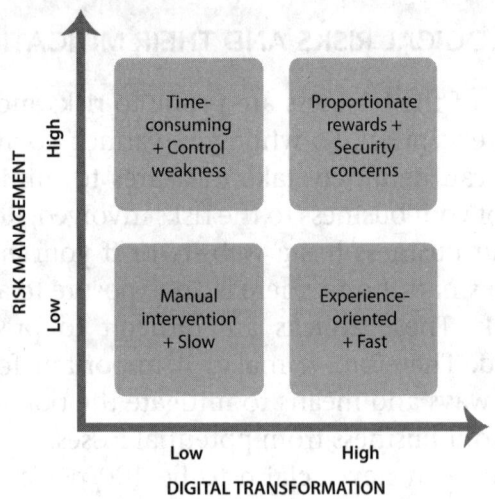

Figure 8.2. Risk Matrix

Risk Mitigation

Here are the steps which you can take to mitigate technological risk:

1. As a first step, identify key risks and measure the probability of occurrence. Also, identify the financial impact it will have on your business.
2. Next, identify any security vulnerabilities and analyse security threats of your business. Evaluate both external risks (such as cybercrime and cyberterrorism) and

internal risks (such as data leakage, authorization, access and controls).

3. Check for the risk of hardware or software failure for your overall business operations. Know the potential consequences of failure.

4. Analyse the risks of outsourcing IT operations such as development, maintenance, network administration and disaster recovery services. It is essential that you choose vendors carefully.

5. Ensure that your computers, servers, data centres and wireless networks are secure. Use periodically updated anti-virus, anti-spyware and firewalls for safety. Regular backups, periodic updates, secure and strong passwords, and understanding legal aspects are essential in mitigating IT risks.

6. Enhance cyber awareness levels within your organization. Although cybersecurity is a complex issue, it should be integrated as part of the culture of your business, as a cyberattack can cause both financial and reputation losses.

7. Train your team in IT policies and procedures. Training can include handling an infected email, protecting the privacy of customer information, actions to be taken in case of an online breach, etc. Build a culture of cybersecurity within your organization.

8. Create a secure online presence (email, website, online banking, social media, etc.) for your business. Prepare an incident management plan which specifies how to handle cyber incidents and provides local resources which can assist.

9. Remote IT security needs to be improved. With the 'work from anywhere' culture catching up, it is a threat to leave valuable business information exposed.

10. It could be prudent to insure your business against IT risks and threats as you may not be able to avoid

them all. Regularly review and update your insurance in relation to the emerging IT risks.

Some businesses, especially the small and medium ones, have preconceived notions or misconceptions about cybersecurity. Highlighting points to overcome the misconceptions below:

- All data is valuable. Protect it appropriately.
- Cybersecurity is not just a technology issue. It is important to educate and train your team on their responsibility to protect the information.
- Cybersecurity does not require a huge financial investment. Efficient policies, restrictive access and training of employees are some effective ways to manage.
- Even by outsourcing to IT operations to a vendor, you still have the onus of protecting the legal and ethical data.
- New software and devices despite being new carry the threat of cybersecurity.

While using technology to grow your business to the next level, remember to take the necessary steps to mitigate the IT-related risks, as otherwise these could cause a huge financial burden on your business.

Watch Out for These Common Mistakes

The common mistakes that businesses commit in connection with technology risks are as follows:

- Not designing and implementing an IT risk mitigation strategy.
- Not implementing an updated anti-virus software, secure passwords and other security measures.

- Not being insured against cyberattacks.
- Lacking preparedness in the case of a cyberattack.
- Not creating an incident management plan in place.

CONTROLLING IT-RELATED COSTS

Cloud computing, process automation, the internet of things (IOT), robotics, etc., are all exciting to have for a business. You are also probably considering these for your business growth. The question to be considered is: Do you have the financial resources for it? Further, most of these are not just a one-time cost. They have recurring costs as well in the form of maintenance costs, connectivity costs, licence costs and such other related costs. So while you are contemplating implementing any of these, you need to take into account the entire cost and also think of it in the long term (both the benefits arising and the costs involved).

While you can use technology to reduce your costs, IT costs by themselves can form a large part of your total expenses. Unless prudence is adopted, this line item can drain away all your profits.

Here are some guidelines to help you control these costs:

1. A good way for you to get started in controlling and managing your IT-related costs would be to get started with a detailed study of your IT requirements. Consult with experts or advisors if required.
2. Based on the study, prepare an IT budget. This will give you the necessary clarity as well as the visibility to know your financial requirements.
3. If you feel that the total amount of the IT budget is well within your financial means, you can proceed with it or else you can follow the steps below.

4. Revisit the IT budget—list down the benefits of each line item.
5. Basis the benefits, segregate them into the following:
   a. Urgent and important
   b. Not urgent but important
   c. Urgent but not important
   d. Not urgent and not important
6. In case you have doubts, reconfirm with an IT expert on the segregation or else ask your colleague or another senior member of the team to undertake the same exercise of segregation.
7. Based on the final round, pick your decisions on narrowing down the IT spend based on your current financial capabilities.

Apart from the above, you can also perform the return of expense (which was discussed in Chapter 1) and then arrive at the costs you want to incur now versus at a later date or even not incur at all. The IT costs have to commensurate with the size and nature of your business.

If you are in the middle of the technology transformation for business or currently pressed for funds, you may also want to consider the below mentioned points apart from the above.

- Get a complete and holistic understanding of your IT framework and requirements.
- Make financial decisions based on where you can adjust some amounts or suspend particular projects after performing a cost–benefit analysis.
- Reset your governance processes as well as investment decisions based on your financial means.
- Evaluate modifications to IT processes and practices and keep them flexible to manage these with changing times and requirements.

According to Shobhana P. Ravi, Chief IT, Innovation & Learning Officer at TAFE, in this era of transformation, innovation and imagination, digital technologies and IT are the greatest enablers of the same. Such a technology-enabled transformational journey has to be linked to the strategic goals of the organization to create an impact on the business, either to the top line or to the bottom line. One of the key drivers to reduce the IT costs would be the time taken for implementation, which should not exceed a period of six–eight months. Recurring IT costs are required to maintain internal systems and continuously enhance value as well as to leverage on the amount invested.

Digital transformation through digital marketing is happening at a rapid pace. Use of local languages has been a big boost to online sales. Similarly, mobile-enabled apps, going cashless and enabling great user experience through artificial intelligence, machine learning and cutting-edge technologies have been game changers in the technology domain.

Building robust IT systems is a continuous journey. There is someone who always wants to outsmart what is current and therefore seeks loopholes and ways to breach security. India is one of the worst-hit countries by cybercrime. Hence, businesses need to have strong access controls as well as end-point controls from a security perspective to protect the brand and reputation. It is not just the job of the IT team but every member of the organization. Continuous risk assessment and creating user awareness by educating the teams to prevent breaches including the ones arising from emails are essential, failing which there will be a huge cost implication. Further, creating the information rights and right IT governance policies and its implementation for the organization can contribute to better IT controls and minimizing risks.

Organizations want to do more with less—lesser people, lesser investments, etc. RPA is a strong business case for repetitive jobs with high volumes and time-consuming routines. It is good to automate because it offers productivity improvement, quality improvement, error-free work due to minimal human intervention, etc. RPA can be adopted in different areas such as employee on-boarding, HR systems, customer service, product classification, product validation and product categorization, which can save costs when the volumes are high. There are many opportunities that exist. A business has to evaluate the benefits and value of such automation by understanding what is most valuable to the organization in terms of its growth strategy. Risk of technology obsolescence exists, and therefore IT value drivers and impact to business need to be assessed. IT payback should be at the earliest, considering the rapid changes in technology.

It is a good practice to mutually benchmark IT processes with other organizations and learn from each other. Using standard frameworks that are available such as ISO 27001, ITIL and CMMI helps. Providing an efficient service desk, tracking internal tickets, ensuring customer satisfaction levels, measuring key metrics and tools are ways to ensure efficiency in IT. IT has to co-create along with the business to deliver value.

S. No.	Topic	Current Level	Proposed Level	Actions to be Taken	Financial Impact (on Top Line/ Bottom Line/ Cash Flow)	Non-financial Impact (on Security, data, IT Efficiency, etc.)
1	Corrective measures taken from the MIS data					
2	Steps to be taken from social media analytical tools					
3	Prepare checklist parameters for technological transformation					
4	Assess steps of technological transformation for business growth					
5	Update the IT security systems					
6	Define the preventive measures for the IT systems					
7	Circulate the cyber-resilient policy within the organization					
8	State the steps to mitigate technological risks					

(Continued)

S. No.	Topic	Current Level	Proposed Level	Actions to be Taken	Financial Impact (on Top Line/ Bottom Line/ Cash Flow)	Non-financial Impact (on Security, data, IT Efficiency, etc.)
9	Evaluate the IT requirements of your organization and prepare the IT budget accordingly to reduce IT costs					
10	Scrutinize the need for RPA, IoT, cloud computing, etc., for your business					
11	Prepare cost–benefit analysis of your IT requirements					
12	Educate your teams on cybersecurity					
13	Decipher the past data and trends with the help of technology					
14	Identify areas where technology can speed up your processes/production					
15	State necessary precautionary IT security measures					

Watch Out for These Common Mistakes

The common mistakes that businesses commit when it comes to controlling IT-related costs are as follows:

- Not changing with the current times and therefore not assessing requirements.
- Not implementing an IT governance framework with policies and procedures that need to be followed.
- Not preparing an IT budget and/or not monitoring the actuals with the budget.
- Not evaluating all options of how technology can be used to reduce costs.
- Not differentiating IT expenses as urgent/important and planning accordingly.

Build Your IT Action Plan

We are in the digital era, and it is good to take advantage of technology, which will help your business to grow.

Rank your current level under each line as Low or Average or Good or Great. Arrive at the desired level and the actions that will get you to the desired level. Measure the financial impact of the action on the top line or bottom line or cash flow. State the non-financial impact of the action. If a topic is not applicable for your business, skip that and move on to the next. To prioritize your action plan, segregate between 'must-have' and 'desirable' actions.

Thoughts for Reflection/Action

- What are the ways in which you can enhance business efficiencies with the help of technology?
- What are the steps you have taken for your business to mitigate technological risks?
- What are the security measures and internal controls put in place to minimize the chances of a cyberattack of your organization?
- How are you controlling the IT costs? What are the processes in place?
- Design a BCP and DRP for your business. Review and update them periodically.

LEADERS SPEAK

IT Is a Business Enabler
Interview of Mr Anand Gonibeedu, India Chief Information Officer, Mondelez International

BUSINESS GAINS WITH IT

The IT function is no longer considered a cost centre. In today's world, the consumerization of IT has allowed different levels of technology adoption which are possible. Cloud, software as a service (SaaS), infrastructure as a service, etc., offer flexibility to organizations to plan their IT infrastructure. IT is not just a cost but an investment, owing to the value which is being delivered.

Regarding recurring IT costs, a business has to define the right cost, how to measure it and what the acceptable norms are. It is useful to benchmark itself with the industry. For example, in the FMCG industry, the range of IT spend could be between 0.8 per cent and 1.2 per cent of net revenue, whereas in the telecom sector the range could be between 3 per cent and 4 per cent in the Indian context. IT costs are like a sine curve year on year because there are years of investment where the cost is high, followed by years of recovery in terms of value from the investment. IT is like a business within a business. The productivity agenda of a business is to reduce costs through economies which could arise within the network, within the processing power or from storage. Hence, as usage of technology increases, costs shrink, and this cost is ploughed back as an investment. Funding IT investment through savings is a strategy which can be adopted. An organization has to clearly define the value needed from the IT function. Along with the recurring IT costs, there is also an associated value added to the cost.

The technology and digital programme need to be embedded in the organization's strategy. The IT function should be considered a business enabler. There are multilayer offerings with different options (which can be used to the advantage of the business) such as:

- Choosing a suitable path which helps the business to scale in terms of benefits
- Eliminating IT legacy costs
- Executing required transformation to set up for the future

If the business is stuck with old technologies and does not keep track of the latest technologies, it risks operations in terms of continuity and security.

CYBERSECURITY

IT risks in the form of viruses in the dark web will remain and continue to grow. As these are unavoidable, organizations need to manage them. Cybersecurity risk is similar to any other business risk. Host of technological options to protect against these threats exist like upgrading tech stack to availability of cybersecurity tools. However, majority of the cybersecurity threats come from the human angle like employees not understanding these risks and falling prey to these attacks. Therefore, enhancing employee awareness is crucial to prevent incurring of extra costs.

DATA SECURITY

Data is the new oil! It outlives the IT applications as well as organizations. Data is created at a rapid pace. Organizations must plan to classify data as confidential data (like product formula or manufacturing cost structure, etc.), restricted use data and public use data. A data framework needs to be created which the data security program can address. For data security, there is no one size that fits all. When security systems are in place, threat of data leakage by uninformed employees who are unaware of their actions is minimized. Data leakage happens because of lack of awareness as they do not know how to deal with data. Tools to prevent data leakage and for data encryption are available, which can be used. Data stewards are required to ensure data integrity as well as against data corruption and prevention of value deterioration. Data policy framework needs to ensure that it gains the trustworthiness of the users.

Digital transformation is an important element to assess the impact of the change caused by technology, on employees and customers. Transformations could fail if these are not focused on training and upskilling employees on change management.

IT MANAGEMENT

IT can be managed in any of the following ways:

- Outsourcing the IT function and keeping it thin
- Internal captive centres or shared services centre for building a scale of multiple business units.
- Hybrid approach wherein IT is partly outsourced and the balance is managed internally

The choice of the above depends on the size and financial budget of the company. Driving efficiencies is possible with scale in any of these above models.

IT EFFICIENCY

IT spend on technological enhancements and digital work needs to be done efficiently by implementing the right tools at the right cost levels. IT has a lag effect because the investment happens in year one and benefits are seen in the subsequent years. Technology is too important to be left only to the IT department. Business leaders need to be involved and understand these tools to drive digital transformation. They need to go through a learning curve to increase their levels of IT awareness. Technology can provide the biggest impact by improving costs, improving consumer experience, creating consumer value, new business models, etc. Business leaders have to take ownership of digital. IT has to be a business agenda item and to be included as part of the business strategy.

09

LEVERAGE ON
FINANCE TO SCALE

CORE OF THE FINANCE FUNCTION: FOCUS ON FUNDS, FIGURES, FEASIBILITY AND FIDUCIARY ASPECTS

Finance is the backbone of any industry, however big or small. One of the common reasons many businesses fail is due to lack of proper financial management. By focusing on the financial aspect of your business, you stand to improve your business profits.

What are the main financial aspects that you should focus on? Like the five elements of nature (space, fire, air, earth and water), the following are the five elements of finance which can help your business to perform well financially.

1. *Space:* Like how there is no end to space, your business revenue can be so vast, having no limits to the growth of your business *top line*. So the space element of finance is revenue. Reflect on the various ways to grow your top line.

2. *Fire:* If your business does not meet sufficient margins, then you feel like your business is on fire! Therefore, simply stated, business *margins* are the fire element. Think about the ways you can achieve better margins.

3. *Air:* We cannot live even for a moment without air! So the air equivalent of your business is indeed *cash*, as you cannot do business without money. Cash is oxygen for your business. Ensure there are no cash shortages in your business.

4. *Earth:* The fourth element is earth, and what I would like to equate it to are the *resources* of your business. Without the requisite resources such as capital, assets, technology and customers, your business may not succeed as well. You need to nurture and nourish them for better growth.

5. *Water:* The essential one! I relate this element with people—your *team* as they are the ones who can deliver operational *efficiency* in your business. They are the key, as they are the ones who make the business. Even if you are a solopreneur, you are the most essential element of the business.

Based on the above, I would encourage you to take a moment and think on the following:

- How are you making the most of the five business finance elements in your business?
- What is your strategy to grow these five elements?
- How would you leverage these five elements to gain the most for your business?

Take stock and burn the financial inefficiencies in your organization. Let the virtues of your business triumph. Some of the financial inadequacies you can get rid of for peaking the financial potential of your business are as follows:

- Cash mismanagement
- Incorrect pricing
- Lack of financial strategy
- Not controlling costs
- Financial indiscipline and non-compliance

- Premature scaling
- Wasting efficiencies of human capital
- Resource misutilization
- Non mitigation of risks
- Poor financial management

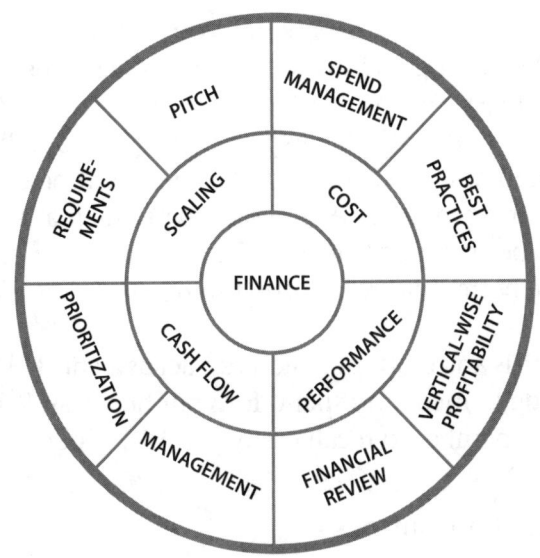

Figure 9.1. Profit Hack Wheel of the Finance Function

By efficiently handling the money matters of your business, you would feel in better control of the financial affairs of your business. So in this chapter, let us check on the following financial aspects, which can help in the financial growth of your business.

1. How to control the costs of your business and manage the spend?
2. How to track the financial performance of your business?
3. How to manage your cash flow?
4. What do you need to do from the finance perspective to scale your business?

The answers to the questions in the previous page are collated together and are represented as the profit hack wheel of the finance function in Figure 9.1.

SPEND MANAGEMENT

During challenging times, what you could control is the spend. Depending on how well your business is performing and the quest for profit, you can manage to control the cost effectiveness of the expenses as per your business requirements. If a business exists, there will be expenses. By exhibiting prudence in your expense management, you will be in a position to take charge of the expenses and have better control on the financial situation of your business.

Here is an acronym which can act as a checklist before you decide to incur any spend for your business. What you need to remember to recall easily is CARE, where

C stands for Control
A stands for Alternative
R stands for Required
E stands for Enhance

- C: Control

Is there a way you can control the amount which is being spent? What are the control mechanisms in place so that the expense does not become too huge to manage? For example, let's say that your business provides food reimbursement to staff who work late. Would you reimburse their food bills if they ate at a five-star hotel? Would you reimburse their bills if they claimed every day? How do you know the food bill is only the cost of their food and not their friends as well? So how are you controlling this spend? You probably want to set limits, have an approval mechanism in place, mention about the food reimbursement in your policy document, etc. In other words, what are the various steps you are taking to control your costs.

- A: Alternative

What are the alternatives to the expense under consideration? What is the current market price for that expense? Have you evaluated other options which are cost-effective? What about comparative quotes? For instance, if you are considering getting health insurance for your employees, you may have evaluated different options from insurance agents. Have you also evaluated if procuring insurance directly from an insurance company is better for you? Remember that while cost is important, cost alone need not be the deciding criterion. Continuing with the same example, if you feel that routing the insurance from an agent is better because you are understaffed and the agent liaises with the insurance company for your claims, etc., then you feel that it is better to route the insurance through an agent. So while evaluating alternatives, look at the holistic picture.

- R: Required

Is the spend which you are considering even required? What are the possibilities for you to do away with the spend? Giving you an example again. In an MNC, for a few years, to encourage team bonding, each month they used to take the employees out for lunch to a five-star restaurant. This practice not only affected productivity but also didn't make the team bonding better. Hence, the management decided to do away with this expense. Thus, questioning the requirement of an expense can be a reality check.

- E: Enhance

By incurring a particular spend, how is it enhancing the value of your business? What are the benefits the business obtains by incurring a particular spend? For instance, the subsidiary of a foreign company had an expatriate CEO who loved flowers. So each morning his office was filled with few exclusive flower arrangements. What started as an initiative to please that CEO was trickled to almost the entire office having beautiful flowers in their flower vases. This tradition continued even after the expatriate went back to his home country. While flowers are beautiful, was it adding value to the business? The successor CEO realized that the cumulative expense of these flower bouquets could rather be spent in paying better bonuses to the staff or some other worthwhile expense for the business and did away with the flower culture.

Thus, by being watchful of your expenses, especially during challenging times, you will be able to minimize the expenses of your business. All that is required is to pause and check on the above parameters, and if you are fulfilled with it, you can proceed with the expense.

> If you can take specific measures to bring down your fixed overheads or save in your cost of production, the amount immediately translates into growing your profit margins. One per cent saved in fixed overheads means one per cent increase in the bottom line.

Based on the above parameters of CARE, once you are convinced that you need to incur a particular expense, you can run it past another checklist. This can be useful when you want to curb your expenses. This checklist—ABCDEFG—is easy to remember.

A. *Assess:* Assess the need for the expense and evaluate benefits.
B. *Budget:* Validate if the particular expense has been budgeted for and if you are within the set budget. If there is no budget, check if there is a possibility to swap it with any other expense line in the budget.
C. *Check:* Check if you can negotiate further on the price, quantity and quality and get any other benefits. Check whether the price and the purchasing terms are in line with the industry standards.
D. *Defer:* Is it possible to postpone and defer the expense to a later date and time period? May be, by then, the need may also recede. Explore this possibility.
E. *Effective:* Justify how the spend is effective for the business or making lives easier or faster for your team.
F. *Feasible:* Is the expense affordable by your business? Is it within your purchasing power?
G. *Goal:* Lastly, is the spend aligned with regard to the overall goals of the business that you want to achieve?

Healthy Finance Practices

Apart from these, here are some healthy practices which your business can implement from the finance perspective:

Internal Controls

State the internal controls which are prevalent within your organization. Who has what authority? Who is authorized to sign on behalf of your organization? Who has the authority to approve what in your business? Who takes the business decisions? What are the approval limits for each person? Check for any loopholes in the system and get them plugged.

Your business should not be people-dependent but process-dependent. To give you an example, an accountant had missed remitting the tax within the due date as he was preoccupied with few other internal issues. Instead of firing the accountant for missing the due date, the entrepreneur set the internal process right by forming a system-generated checklist, which would prompt for payment before the due date.

Audit

Auditors can be both internal and external, depending on the size and nature of your business operations. Implementing the suggestions and recommendations from the auditors can help you with the internal control weakness as well as setting right any internal inefficiencies, if any. Also, frauds, thefts and errors, if any, are likely to be unearthed in the audit process. Maintain necessary documentation to have the audit trail.

Zero-based Budgeting

Zero-based budgeting (ZBB) helps to ensure that the costs are kept at a minimum. Usually, once the budgets are firmed up, the departments' budgets are usually shared with the respective department heads. This usually sets the precedence for spending for the year under review.

ZBB starts with a zero base. Just because a cost was incurred in the previous years, does it mandatorily mean it has to be incurred in the current period as well? Therefore, all expenses must be justified and analysed for each period by the department head, and a conscious business decision needs to be arrived at.

The advantages of resorting to ZBB within your organization is that it helps in lowering the costs, offers flexibility in budgets and focuses on the core operations and disciplined execution. On the flip side, sometimes, they can be manipulated to one's advantage and could also create a bias in short-term planning. So prudence needs to be applied on a case-to-case basis.

Business Policies

Business policies are intended to specify the boundaries of your business activities. They help you to regulate business operations and aid in decision-making and efficient management of business. It is best to have the policies documented and update them periodically in line with the growth of the business.

The business's policies must specify the framework on how to deal with challenges and ensure that business operations are carried out in a fair and consistent manner within the entity. Some essential policies you can have are leave policy, travel policy, information security policy, whistle blower policy, HR policy, vendor empanelment policy and so on.

Procedures

Procedure is a documented description of the prescribed course(s) of action or process(es) to enable adherence to the business's policies. It details the path to be taken to execute a task. Examples of procedures include purchase procedure, invoicing procedure and payroll procedure, which reveal the step-by-step action to be performed towards the desired result.

Legal and Compliance Matters

With regard to compliance matters, there should be absolutely no compromise. It is extremely important to adhere to the compliance aspects as per the specified rules and regulations, as applicable to your organization. While the cost of compliance may not have a major financial impact, the cost of non-compliance is high. Apart from penalties, interest charges and so on, it could sometimes also result in imprisonment (depending on the nature of non-compliance). Further, you could lose out on funding and other opportunities due to non-compliance issues. It is better to be safe than sorry.

Finance Dashboard

Have a complete overview of the business performance by reviewing the finance dashboard periodically. The dashboard serves as a quick visual comparison of key performance parameters of your business. It also provides a glimpse of all important business data at one go, including the costs that you are wanting to have a keen eye upon. You can design and customize the dashboard the way you want.

Industry-specific Best Practices

Depending on the industry your business is in, you can follow the industry-specific best practices and also learn from your peers in the industry. For instance, if you are in the IT industry, following the industry average on various matters such as attrition ratio, cost of recruitment, cost of training and per diem allowance, can be in line with the general industry norms.

Watch Out for These Common Mistakes

The common mistakes that businesses commit regarding spend management are as follows:

- Not thinking about the financial repercussions or implications before deciding on a spend.
- Spending on an impulse without being conscious of costs.
- Not thinking about the long-term impact of the expense.
- Not following industry-specific best practices.
- Doing a post-mortem instead of taking preventive measures on cost management.

FINANCIAL PERFORMANCE

Many entrepreneurs and business owners being extremely busy in the business operations do not pay heed to the financial affairs. The most common reply is that the accountant or the auditor will handle the finance-related matters. While the accountant, auditor, advisor, consultant, coach, etc., can guide you or help you overcome your business finance challenges, remember that the onus lies on you as the business belongs to you. While you can hear the advice and take the required coaching, it is up to you to take the right financial decisions.

The financial performance of your business is a lot dependent on the business decisions that you take. While making the business decisions, you ought to think of the impact on the financial situation of your business and the financial impact it would cause and then take the call. That way, you are fully conscious of taking the right business decisions. Many people tend to make decisions based on emotions. While we are all humans and driven by emotions, it is also important to take decisions by being rational and with full awareness. Leave aside the assumptions and preconceived notions while making the decisions.

For the financial performance of your business to get better, you need to review the financial statements periodically and take necessary actions to improve the financial performance of the business. Here are some of the key items that you need to review:

Budget

Budgets act as financial guides and help in measuring the business's actual financial performance. Unfavourable deviations from the budget must be scrutinized, and efforts must be made right away to get back on track, in line with the budget. Some of the different types of budgets that can be used as per your business requirements are as follows:

- *Master budget:* It tracks the complete financial activity of your business.
- *Sales budget:* It takes into account the sales revenue, direct selling expenses, sale quantities, sale values, etc. Also included are the season-related sales, etc.
- *Production budget:* It is prepared in relation to the sales budget. The items considered for this budget are material, labour, direct overheads, etc.
- *Cash budget:* It is based on cash in and out.
- *Zero-based budget:* It starts with zero base and does not consider the previous year numbers.
- *Capital budget:* This revolves around the fixed asset requirements and includes the acquisition cost as well as maintenance of the fixed asset for a long term or life of the asset.
- *Operating budget:* This budget is based on the day-to-day operational requirement for a period of say a year.
- *Financial budget:* This is purely based on the financial requirements of your business for long-term as well as short-term financial needs.

- *Static budget:* This type of budget is a fixed budget, and no deviations to this budget irrespective of any external or internal changes that happens are accommodated.
- *Rolling budget:* This is the opposite of a static budget. Continuous budgets are prepared on quarterly, half-yearly and annual bases.

Forecast

Periodically (say, every quarter), you need to update your budget and prepare a forecast or projected profit and loss, which will provide a realistic year-end performance of your business. This is not mandatory but would help you assess your company's performance and serve as a guide on the necessary steps to be taken and ensure that your business is on top of the game. Forecast is prepared based on the past and the assumptions for the future. Projections are prepared on the hypothetical course of action which the business might have.

Monthly Financials

Reviewing your monthly financial statements is important as it gives you a sense of how the business is performing. By reviewing, it reveals to you what is going well for the business and what are the areas which can be improved. By reading it, you can work on strategies to improve your margins and get better financial results.

Financial Analysis

Different types of financial analyses for enhancing financial performance of your business can be performed, for example, variance analysis, risk analysis, profitability analysis, efficiency analysis, financing capacity analysis, loan analysis, ratio analysis and the like. Financial analysis is a tool which helps you to evaluate the performance of your business based on various key parameters. It helps in cost control, cost reduction and cash management. It could reveal to you the lacuna in the system and further encourage you to dig deeper into the performance and plug the holes. This helps propel your business towards better performance and take necessary corrective steps.

Cash Status

Reviewing the cash balance and knowing the amount of cash which is there in your business at any point in time will help you make the right and timely financial decisions. We shall explore more of this in the next few pages.

Profitability

If you are manufacturing, say, five different products or rendering various services for different verticals, it would be a financially healthy habit to compute the product profitability or segmental profitability. It is important to undertake this exercise in order to know which product or segment gives you the maximum yield, highest profit generator or, for that matter, which customer contributes the most towards profitability. Not only does it provide you clear visibility in terms of individual financial performance, but it also helps you understand which areas you need to focus upon.

It aids in planning ahead in terms of the product or service you need to sell more of in order to generate better profits or throws light on either increasing the selling price of a particular product or upscaling efforts in sales and so on, if a particular product is not selling as per your target.

Financial Metrics

Business metrics are performance indicators of your business. It involves a detailed analysis of your financial results and displays measurable values which show the progress of your business. At times, they act as reminders to let you know how far you are from achieving your business goals for that specific period. You can have specific metrics from the cost management perspective, for example, connectivity cost per employee and cost of customer acquisition, which are relevant to your business.

Seven deadly sins of financial management are as follows:
1. Poor cash management and no financial review
2. Not plugging revenue leakages
3. Spending without measuring the benefit
4. Not building sufficient cash reserves
5. People-dependent and not process-dependent
6. Taking loans that do not build wealth or increase income in the long term
7. Not getting sufficient ROI

Watch Out for These Common Mistakes

The common mistakes that businesses commit regarding financial performance are as follows:

- Not reviewing the financial performance of the business on a regular and periodic basis.
- Thinking that finance is the responsibility of only the finance department.
- Not getting into the details and reasons of the variance analysis.
- Neglecting to prepare the forecasts and projections.
- Not strategizing enough about the corrective measures to be taken to improve the financial performance.

MANAGING THE CASH FLOW

Cash is oxygen for any business. While you can control your cash outflow, you may not have 100 per cent control on the cash inflow. The cash situation can sometimes be challenging. Some entrepreneurs I spoke to mentioned how they have sleepless nights wondering about how they would manage to pay their current month's salaries and so on. However, if you plan your cash properly, you will have no more sleepless nights.

There have been many well-known companies in the past which have filed for bankruptcy. Take the instance of Jet Airways, which was once the largest carrier of passengers. Some of the reasons why Jet Airways went bankrupt included cut-throat price wars, high operational costs and huge debts. While it is not uncommon for businesses to get into financial crises, lack of timely action exacerbates the problem. With better planning, you can protect yourself from the cash crunch. By looking ahead and planning for contingencies, a business can mitigate some of the cash flow risk.

Cash Profit versus Book Profit

Despite your business performing a set of actions, the book profit of your business and the cash profit are different. Why? Because the cash profit takes into account only the cash transactions, resulting in the difference arising on account of reasons such as depreciation, prepayments, timing difference and accruals. As an entrepreneur, both are important for you because the cash profit keeps your business going, and the book profit is what your bankers, investors and other external agencies consider.

To manage your cash flow better, here are some pointers which you can follow for your business. Let me share another acronym here. CASH is the acronym for cash flow management. What does it stand for?

C: Collect on time
A: Anticipate your cash inflow and outflow
S: Systematically monitor
H: Habit of reserves

- C: Collect on Time

When the amount is due for collection and it is not yet paid or nearing the end of the credit period given, follow up continuously, send reminders, etc., till the amount is credited. Try to collect your dues well within the time.

- A: Anticipate Your Inflow and Outflow

Based on the past trends, know the amount of money which will be going out and the amount of money which is likely to come in. This will give you better clarity on the financial position and thereby enable you to make right financial decisions.

- **S: Systematically Monitor**

   Get to know the amount of cash you have at your disposal. Monitor if there are any cheques issued which are not yet debited from your bank account and also scrutinize the bank statement for any unknown debits or credits.

- **H: Habit of Reserves**

   Have a habit of creating cash reserves for your business so that during times of emergency, your business does not succumb to the pressure of cash shortage and can survive without hassles.

   Apart from following the above, a few specific areas you can focus on regarding cash management are as follows:

Working Capital Requirements

First, know your working capital requirements so that the business is able to manage from the cash perspective. Like you are already aware, working capital is the difference between the current assets and current liabilities. So you need to focus on each item of the current asset and current liability to strengthen your working capital. Create an action plan for the working capital management. Do not wait till the time the business is pressed for cash. Start taking necessary actions right away. For instance, some measures you could undertake are as follows:

- *From collection perspective:* Collect old dues and reduce the credit period.

- *From the inventory angle:* Remove inventory bottlenecks and reduce the excess quantity of stock in hand.
- *From the supply standpoint:* Reduce lead time and lengthen credit terms.

Advance from Customers

As a best practice to manage your cash better, it is always wise to take an advance from your customer as an upfront payment before you commence working on their assignments/projects. The amount of advance can vary according to several factors, including negotiations with your customer, delivery period, delivery schedule, cash position, rapport with your customer and so on. The underlying idea is that by getting an advance from the customer, you know the order is confirmed. Your working capital is seamless and you have to recover only the balance from your customer. Further, cash advance is also to make sure that the customer takes more accountability and does not cancel or delay the order, further affecting your cash flow.

Review of Receivables

One of the reasons some entities face a cash crunch despite making book profits is because of the status of their receivables. If your collections do not happen on time, your cash inflow is affected and, therefore, there is a good chance that you will face a cash flow deficit. Periodic and regular reviews of your receivable status will help tremendously with your cash flow. Not all businesses will have the fixed routine to pay the amount due without continuous follow-ups. So it is in your own interest that you need to get what is due for your business.

One of the best ways to follow up would be by systematically tracking the collection report periodically. The age analysis of your debtors reveals the position of your receivables. It would be prudent to have a system of sending weekly or time-based reminders to collect the dues.

Bad Debts

You need to take every possible measure to ensure that there are no bad debts, as incurring bad debts do not help your business. Some steps that can act as a useful measure in bad debt collections are as follows:

- As a first step, ensure that your accounts receivable status reflects the correct status.
- Remember that the older the age of the debt, the more difficult is the collection.
- Hence, as soon as an amount becomes due, start following up with your customers through phone calls, emails, formal letters and so on. Depending on the quantity and volume, have a dedicated person/team, if required, to follow up on the collections.
- If you have not received your dues despite umpteen follow-ups, appoint a legal consultant to write demand letters.
- If giving a minor discount to the customer will help the cause (as it is better to forego a small amount rather than the entire debt), do that.
- Come to a consensus with your debtor and agree on a debt recovery plan.
- If you are still unable to recover the debt, appoint a collection agent who can collect on your behalf.
- If none of the above works, you will have to go to the court to recover your dues.

You can also think of creative ways to recover your potential bad debts. For example,

An entrepreneur who was running an advertising agency was owed close to ₹50 lakh by a construction company. The company did not have sufficient liquid funds to pay this amount. After multiple rounds of discussions, finally, the entrepreneur thought of an idea. The construction company had unsold units of an apartment complex they had constructed. The entrepreneur negotiated for one such apartment from the builder as he realized that otherwise, it would take a very long time to recover his dues.

A financially prudent way to handle bad debts would be to start provisioning some amount on a monthly basis so that it doesn't affect your financial statements at the year end. This way, the liability would be spread over months and would not hit you at one go.

Prioritization of Cash Outflow

Controlling the cash out is completely in your hands. Here is a checklist on prioritizing cash out. You can use this checklist when you want to control your cash situation.

- *Business operations:* First settle the dues which are directly in connection with your business operations, so that it generates more money for the business which will enable you to pay the other important dues.
- *Legal:* Prioritize your legal and statutory dues, because failure to comply with legal aspects not only comes with a penalty but could also result in imprisonment. Hence, adhere to the applicable compliances.

- *Investment:* Investing in the procurement of equipment of machinery, which will enhance the business operations, is next in line. It could also be towards building and growing the asset base of your business.
- *Necessary reserves:* Having the necessary reserves which can help your business on a rainy day or in case of an emergency is important. Hence, have liquid reserves (e.g., fixed deposit and liquid funds) which can come in handy at the time of need.
- *General expenses:* All other payouts can be made after the above are managed. It also helps you not to go overboard with your cash, as you have prioritized the important ones first.

This way, you can ensure that the important ones are taken care of, and then with the balance you can plan to pay all the other expenses.

Watch Out for These Common Mistakes

The common mistakes that businesses commit regarding cash flow management are as follows:
- Not assessing the working capital requirements.
- Not preparing debtors age analysis or not having a system to follow up on the money due.
- Not prioritizing the cash payouts.
- Neglecting to prepare cash flow projections for short-term basis.
- Not thinking long term and therefore not creating sufficient liquid reserves for any crisis.

Seven deadly sins of cash management are as follows:

1. Not anticipating cash inflow and outflow
2. Being passive and not following up the amounts due
3. Borrowing to fix cash flow issues instead of addressing the root cause
4. Unaware of the cash runway
5. Not monitoring the movement of funds
6. Not creating cash reserves
7. Not utilizing the cash to generate more cash

FINANCE AND SCALING UP

Your business growth could be organic or inorganic or a combination of both. When the growth is exponential and when the revenue is growing significantly without incurring substantial costs, your business is said to scale. When there is exponential growth, there is a high likelihood of funds which are required.

The finance required could be raised from within the business, can be in the form of a bank loan or a loan taken from family and friends, through investors, etc. If you decide to route the funding requirement from external sources (such as investors and bank), there are few aspects which you need to take into account which could help you in getting these funds in a smooth manner. Let us check what these aspects are.

How to Pitch

If you are approaching investors for funding, you need to prepare a pitch deck. In the first round of pitching, you need to get the attention of the investors within the few minutes which you are allotted. Once you are able to get their interest, then you can get into further details in the subsequent rounds. The preliminary pitch round is important, and I have noticed that many start-ups as well as seasoned entrepreneurs do not succeed in pitching their business ideas to prospective investors.

So here is an easy checklist which will enable you to cover all the important aspects during the time of your pitch. The acronym which you need to remember is PITCH.

P: Problem that is being solved

I: Investment required

T: Team composition

C: Customer and market strategy

H: High level numbers

- P: Problem That Is Being Solved

    Start your pitch by letting your prospective investor know the following:

    ° What is the problem your business is solving?
    ° What is the USP of your business?
    ° How have you got some of your big orders?

- I: Investment Required

    Next talk about the investment amount which is required and how you are planning to utilize the funds. Also, if there are any existing investors, mention about them as well.

- T: Team Composition

    Speak about the team—founders, experts, your coaches, mentors, advisors, etc., and how well you complement each other.

- C: Customer and Market Strategy

  Next share about the profile of your customer, major customers, markets you operate in (and plan to expand to), testimonials received, etc.

- H: High-level Numbers

  Share the high-level financial performance numbers from the recent past along with the projections for the next few years. Also, share in here how the prospective investor will get benefited by becoming an investor in your business.

Funding Requirements

Understand the why and what of your funding requirements. This could be a key propelling factor or else you could be carried away by the fact that funding is a fad. There are advantages and disadvantages of your business getting funded. Prepare a complete financial projection for the next five years to get a clear understanding.

By having the required clarity, vision and a growth path ahead makes it easier for you to assess the funding requirements. Once you are sure about the requirement, evaluate the various options available to fund your business. If you are seeking funding (or a loan), know that like how there are two sides to a coin, funding also has its pros and cons. Take the right decision by being fully aware of the possible consequences.

Top reasons how funding or a loan helps are as follows:

- Your business to scale fast
- Smooth cash flow
- Buy necessary equipment, finance existing loans or invest in future growth

What you must be aware of while seeking funding is as follows:

- You need to part with the equity (i.e., part with some portion of the ownership).
- Sharing of the business profits.
- You are accountable to the investors on the business decisions, business performance, etc.

If you are opting for a loan to grow your business, know that

- The loan interest is a cost which will reduce your profits.
- The monthly loan repayment has an impact on your cash flow.
- You need to offer security/collateral for the loan.

Whichever option you decide on, remember to make your decision with full awareness of the pros and cons.

Some new-generation entrepreneurs think that funding is the only way to grow or else they are under the impression that their business cannot grow anymore. Note that in the past, there have been many businesses which had scaled successfully without being funded. So although funding may help in quick growth, it is not the end all. Be mindful and take the best decision for your business regarding the funding.

Fake Stake Syndrome

This is something you should be watchful of so that you do not fall into this trap. In my own mission to help entrepreneurs achieve financial wellness, a successful tech entrepreneur wanted to know if I knew suitable investors for the business. Having spoken and helped many entrepreneurs, I sensed that there was something more than this the entrepreneur was seeking. The eyes showed a sense of pain, and the voice had despair. Being a coach, I started probing deeper.

As the conversation progressed, the entrepreneur revealed the truth—he sought an investor because of persistent cash flow issues. The entrepreneur admitted that despite running a successful business for the past decade, cash flow was an issue month after month, and the entrepreneur wondered how to pay salaries on time.

It was disturbing emotionally as well, as this issue could not be discussed with the spouse, children, employees or friends. Finally, the entrepreneur poured out the issues to his heart's content and felt much lighter. Being a techie, the entrepreneur admitted that there was no attention to business finance.

I realized that the entrepreneur was falling prey to what I call the 'fake stake syndrome',[1] wherein the entrepreneur is filled with hope that the cash flow issues would vanish, without addressing the root cause of the issue. I wanted the entrepreneur to become aware of this.

As our coaching conversation progressed, many ideas were uncovered. The discussions made the entrepreneur realize the following:

- A new investor would only solve the cash flow issue temporarily.
- What needed to be fixed was a better system of working capital management.
- The revenue model was not right.

So watch out if you are by any chance caught in any such fake syndrome unknowingly.

---

[1] Sangeeta Shankaran Sumesh, *Get High: How to Coach Yourself for High Performance in Your Work* (Chennai: Notion Press, 2020).

S. No.	Topic	Current Level	Proposed Level	Actions to be Taken	Financial Impact (on Top Line/ Bottom Line/ Cash Flow)	Non-financial Impact (on Process, Controls, Policies, etc.)
1	List controls for introduction regarding spend management					
2	Financial best practices for improving financial health					
3	Key metrics for measuring the financial performance					
4	Ways to track cash position and improve liquidity position					
5	Important elements to be featured in the finance dashboard					
6	Actions to be taken from the key ratios					
7	Assess funding requirements					

8	Mitigation plan of financial risks					
9	Steps for prioritization of legal and compliance matters					
10	Decision to be taken based on cash forecast for the next 12 months					
11	Minimum cash reserve strategy					
12	Actions for improving the important ratios					
13	Steps to be taken based on variance analysis					
14	Effects from the implementation of ZBB					
15	New steps to be taken to strengthen internal controls					

Watch Out for These Common Mistakes

The common mistakes that businesses commit regarding funding are as follows:

- Not assessing properly the funding requirements and the plans for its usage.
- Seeking funding for managing the working capital without plugging the root cause issues of cash flow issues.
- Failing to highlight/state explicitly to potential investors 'what's in it for them' or how their investment will multiply.
- Thinking that funding is a one-stop shop to all the cash problems.
- Overstating the net worth of the business for valuation purpose.

Build Your Finance Action Plan

Take charge of the financial situation of your business so that you can make the right business decisions and grow your profits as well as manage your cash position.

Rank your current level under each line as Low or Average or Good or Great. Arrive at the desired level and the actions that will get you to the desired level. Measure the financial impact of the action on the top line or bottom line or cash flow. State the non-financial impact of the action. If a topic is not applicable for your business, skip that and move on to the next. To prioritize your action plan, segregate between 'must-have' and 'desirable' actions.

Thoughts for Reflection/Action

- Study the financial industry trends of your business. Benchmark the current level of your business performance against the industry standards. What is the gap indicating about your business?
- Talk to your industry peers and make a list of the best practices which will help you manage your business more efficiently.
- Based on the vertical-wise profitability, what business decisions would you want to take to improve the overall profitability of your business?
- What steps can you take to improve your cash flow?
- Seek an advisor or a coach who can help your business to progress, grow and scale further.

LEADERS SPEAK

Growth Is the Only Way to Grow
Interview of Mr Venkatesh Viswanathan, Chief Financial Officer, Global Outsourcing, RR Donnelley

RATIOS THAT MATTER

Some key ratios which a business can track to manage their progress to grow the profits would be as follows:

- Revenue generated per employee
- Direct cost as a percentage of revenue
- Labour margin
- Gross margin

- Income from operations as a percentage of revenue (IFO %)

The labour margin is crucial to track for both products and services businesses, and it shows where the businesses energy is being spent, especially where there are many different products to be monitored. By scrutinizing this ratio, a business can decide where to focus on. Labour margin is computed in the following manner:

$$\text{Labour margin} = \frac{(\text{Revenue generated} - \text{Direct labour cost of the revenue thus generated}) \times 100}{\text{Revenue generated}}$$

The direct labour cost includes amounts such as salaries, benefits, overheads, temporary labour costs, project-related travel costs and any other specific costs directly associated with generating the revenue.

The difference between the labour margin and the gross profit is due to the indirect fixed overheads such as rent, utilities, insurance and depreciation. From the gross margin when the selling and administrative costs (like salaries of the sales team and support teams) are reduced, it is what the business is left with as the IFO. Allocating the indirect costs to each project and measuring the project-wise IFO are critical for business decisions, basis which the business can focus on the areas to grow high margins.

Irrespective of having a finance inclination or not, from the balance sheet, an entrepreneur can focus on the following:

- *Working capital:* To check if there is more cash going out than coming in and whether the business is in better control to pay the liabilities.
- *Inventory turnover ratio:* To know the duration during which the inventory can be held so as to convert

the stock into cash. Measure the number of days of inventory outstanding.

- *Debt to total assets ratio:* Profits can either be part of reserves and surplus or to service the debts. Businesses should aim at lowering this curve as this is critical.

TOP-LINE GROWTH

Technology to be leveraged for business growth by factoring in these two parameters:

1. How can the customers' life be made easy with the technological advancements?
2. Enhance the user experience through technology enablement.

Technological advancements will replace the age-old ways of providing services, however good these are. Invest in making necessary changes in creating the required solutions for the customers who are ready for customer adaptation. This will enable to grow customers as well as retain the existing customers.

FINANCIAL EFFICIENCIES

To maximize financial efficiencies of a service-oriented business, the business has to measure productivity. To measure productivity, calculate if the business can get more done with the same cost and same resources.

A formula to compare the efficiency level would be to measure the following.

Take the previous year's direct cost as a percentage of revenue. Let's say this is X. Multiply this to the current year's revenue and let us call this Y.

If the difference between X and Y pertains to anything over and above the wage inflation, it requires the labour mix to be adjusted, as it determines the financial efficiency levels. Check on the span of control and the ratio of freshers versus experienced resources and adjust accordingly. The ideal labour mix must deliver client satisfaction, employee satisfaction and financial efficiency to grow profits.

For manufacturing organizations, the focus should be on minimizing wastages arising from the conversion of inventory to the saleable product. Efforts need to be taken to reduce the carrying costs of inventory as well as labour mix.

Investing in sales and marketing team and measuring their output are vital. Check whether this ratio as a percentage of sales is increasing or decreasing. As a thumb rule, it would be ideal if the sales team is able to deliver at least –six–eight times of their cost as revenue for SMEs as a minimum.

Depending on whether a business is in a sellers' market or buyers' market, the business can get comfortable with their working capital requirements. If the business is anticipating extra growth in the form of new orders and is not in a position to finance this growth, then the business should opt for term loans and project loans after comparing the cost of capital.

The MSME businesses which are struggling with the cash flow can consider repurchase of invoices like a bill discounting option. This can be planned as per the financial requirements. Know the difference if the business is struggling for survival or struggling for growth, based on which the decision for borrowings can be taken.

FINANCIAL RISK

To minimize the financial risk, check on the following factors:

- What kind of liability is the business exposed to with the clients?
- How is the business being protected?
- Restrict the liability to a certain amount through the contract.
- Sometimes customers seek unlimited liability, which the business has to watch out.
- Ensure that the intellectual property remains with the business and the customers do not take it away.
- Workmen and assets are to be covered for all possible business insurances as the cost of replacement is very high.

CASH MANAGEMENT

'Collect early pay late' is probably the easiest way in theory and most difficult one to practise. In practical terms, cash collection needs to be a team responsibility. There could be conflicts on follow-ups with the customer between the sales team and the finance team. Usually, the agenda of the sales team is to grow the business and hence a dedicated resource from the finance team can send gentle reminders to the customers on upcoming dues, so that before an amount becomes overdue, the business is already following up for collections. Further, a good way to manage the debt could be to leverage the position in the industry, for example, whether the business has the ability to dictate and negotiate with vendors.

The top three actions points could be the following:

1. Negotiate better payment terms which can go a long way for the liquidity of a business.
2. Talk to the customers and reduce the collection cycle, say, from 45 days to 30 days. Similarly, when renewing contracts with vendors, negotiate for terms like better credit terms, etc. By asking this with all the vendors and few obliging, it will go a long way with the cash status.
3. Ability to quickly convert inventory to debtors to cash will help the cash cycle.

Thus, the areas for prime focus for better cash management are credit terms, payment terms and inventory to cash cycle.

ROLE OF FINANCE TEAM

The role of the finance team has evolved from book keeping to invoicing to being a business partner. The finance team is the custodian of all the information. Every business transaction gets converted to a value, and the information of the same lies with the finance team. The finance team has the vantage point by providing the right information in determining the right pricing, related commercial aspects, investment requirements, etc.

Apart from contributing to the business growth by providing commercial support, the finance team should also educate the operations team on the costs, ratios, financial metrics to track, etc. The team should further help differentiate the operations team between the controllable costs and non-controllable costs. This will help in margin improvement and business sustenance.

LONG-TERM GROWTH

Growth is key. How the business grows is what matters the most. Without the top-line growth, by resorting to cost adjustment and changes, the business can still maintain the similar margin levels. However, this cannot be the long-term solution for growth. Investment should provide the necessary returns. Focus on business strengths and savviness to the market trends pave the way to the growth. Growth is the only way to grow.

10

ACCELERATING FINANCIAL GROWTH

A business can grow its top line year on year, establish new branches, increase its customer base, etc., but if it does not focus on the bottom line and cash situation, then its financial stability is impacted. Thus, as the business owner or business head, you need to ensure that the business is focusing on the right and important parameters.

Being a successful IT entrepreneur running an IT company called Tenth Planet, Kumaran Mani shared that he thought he had learned the nuances about all facets of running a successful business. He decided to venture into restaurant business and make it a success.

It was opened in a prime location with grand interiors with celebrities for the inauguration. Yet the sales did not pick up. New range of snacks were introduced—still, the sales were poor. From the operations perspective, there were challenges to find qualified managers, chefs and reliable billing counter person. Due to poor internal controls, equipment and ingredients were stolen.

Apart from these challenges, Chennai Metro work commenced and right at the entrance a big barrier was put up for 12 months and the restaurant had to be closed.

Kumaran decided to sell the restaurant as he incurred a huge loss.

Today at the same place runs a coffee house with many quick bites, lunch items and drinks, and this business is flourishing. This left Kumaran with some valuable lessons such as

- Fix the right pricing.
- It is important to have the right product mix.
- Choose the right target customers.
- Don't invest heavily on non-core items.
- Appoint the right people.

Focus on your niche and diversification may not be necessary, concludes Kumaran.

Apart from pivoting on each of the different business functions like we have seen so far in this book, what else can your business do to grow the profits? Here are few other pointers to help the financial growth of your business.

FOCUSED PROFITS

The key to building a business with sound profits as well as good liquidity depends on the focus areas. Apart from focusing on your customers, focusing on your core business principles, having well-defined processes and driving efficiencies internally would contribute to better margins. Some pointers on this are as follows:

- Principle
  - When the principle on pricing is right, the top line continues to grow.

- By applying the principle of prudence, the expenses can be minimized.
- Defining the right principle of liquidity, the cash position can be managed.

- Process
  - When the set processes are well designed, revenue grows with time.
  - If the processes are crafted carefully, expenses can be controlled.
  - By monitoring the process of cash, cash management is ensured.

- Efficiency
  - Developing the segmental efficiency of the business contributes to revenue.
  - By measuring the returns on expenses, the expenses can be controlled.
  - By efficiently forecasting the cash, cash crisis can be avoided.

The above translates into the understated 3×3 matrix, which helps in profit maximization based on the focus areas.

		PROFIT		
		Revenue	Expense	Cash
FOCUS	**Principle**	Pricing	Prudence	Liquidity
	Process	Timing	Controls	Monitoring
	Efficiency	Segmental	Returns	Forecast

FOREST PRINCIPLE

Irrespective of the nature and size of your business, what are the sources of your revenue? Is it primarily from just one main source? Are you relying only on your core business? Many well-established businesses miss out on the importance of having multiple sources of revenue or sometimes fail to have a revenue strategy in place. Take the case of Toys 'R' Us, which had to shut shop as they succumbed to competition.

On the other hand, consider McDonald's for instance. Where do you think it gets its revenue from? If you thought it is only from Big Mac or Chicken McNuggets, you are mistaken! Apart from these, McDonald's has other sources which contribute to its huge profits, the sources being rent, royalty income and franchise fees.

When you work on your revenue to have a wide variety of sources like a forest, you are stepping up your revenue and grow. Devise ways and means to inculcate this forest principle in your business.

So for the business to stay alive for long, it is essential for it to grow in more than one way. The first step in business growth is revenue. While revenue growth cannot guarantee profits, the more the revenue, the higher the probability of increased profits. Take a moment to reflect on the following questions:

- What is your plan to increase your sources of revenue?
- How do you intend on achieving revenue growth?
- What is the impact of the revenue growth on your profits?

Irrespective of the nature of your business, here is a simple step-by-step guide to help you formulate your revenue strategy.

STEP 1: BULL'S EYE

While businesses may have revenue growth targets, the sweet spot in focus is what I am referring to as the bull's eye. To achieve your bull's eye, you must ensure that your revenue is higher than your costs by the desired profit.

So if you want to achieve a profit of 100 and your costs are 1,000, then your revenue should be at 1,100, which should be your focus.

Alternatively, if you know your costs are at 2,000 and you want a profit margin of 10 per cent on costs, then the revenue should be at 2,200. So it is essential to arrive at your desired target.

Now that you know what you want to achieve, make a basic plan on how you will go about achieving it.

STEP 2: PRICING

It is important to arrive at the right pricing for your offering as it boosts your revenue. Especially if you are a new player in the market, it is vital for you to know the best price which you can sell your products/services at. While the pricing is directly under your control, some factors are beyond your control such as inflation, perceived value by your potential customers and market value of your offering. You can refer to Chapter 3 for the different ways of pricing strategy.

STEP 3: SUSTAINABILITY

Once your pricing is in place, ensure that your revenue is sustainable. Ask yourself how you can set the revenue in auto pilot mode so that you have a recurring amount as revenue every month. Your main source of revenue or main stream revenue should ensure that your business is sustainable.

What can you do to get to that level? While it is good to rely on the 80/20 principle, what happens if your major customer is no longer your customer for whatever reasons? It may be good to have an alternative in place.

STEP 4: OPTIMIZATION

Your business may have many resources such as human resources, machinery, equipment and office space. As an entrepreneur, how are you leveraging on these to optimize your revenue? Yet another important resource that most people tend to overlook is time. How are you keeping a tab of time and its impact on your revenue? Remember that the more the delay, higher your costs and later your revenue.

It is essential for a prudent entrepreneur to utilize all your available resources extensively, thereby leading to your revenue growth.

STEP 5: SCALABILITY

Your revenue has to be scalable. You can look at various ways of scaling such as cross-selling to your existing customers and to newer ones, and entering new markets and newer territories for your growth. Have you considered mergers, acquisitions, collaboration, and forward and backward integration to ensure growth?

Should your business grow exponentially, are you in a position to handle the inorganic growth? Your revenue strategy needs to feature the scalability aspect.

STEP 6: DIFFERENT SOURCES

When digital cameras were introduced, within no time the non-digital cameras were gone. To avoid falling into such traps, like McDonald's, it is crucial to have revenue coming from various sources, irrespective of the fact that you only have one core business or many businesses. Since some businesses like to specialize only in one particular type of offering and offer it as a niche rather than diversifying, what can be the other potential sources of revenue? If you do not want to diversify, other sources of revenue could be interest income, investment income, rental income, etc.

What will happen to your business if the core activity of your business is shut down? By having multiple sources of revenue, you will have something to fall back on and also give you time to recover and get back into business at the earliest.

STEP 7: INNOVATE

What are you doing differently for your customer base to grow? What will make your potential customers flock to you? By spending time on this, you can identify your USP. By doing something differently or offering freebies to your customers, you may have a strong potential to grow. Classic examples of this are most social media platforms like Facebook and also portals like Paytm, where the masses tend to utilize these platforms. There is no charge and at the same time, the business grows rapidly.

What is the problem that your business is solving? Think about how your business can address the unmet needs of your potential customer.

STEP 8: AWARENESS

What have you done to create awareness about your offering? If someone is looking for a product or service similar to yours, how will they know that you are offering it? A good idea would be to make sure that you have a good marketing plan in place and thereby convert leads to potential customers. If your offering is unique, the prospect may not even be aware that such a product or service exists.

So what are you doing to reach your potential customers? Reflect upon creating your brand and creating awareness to your target audience about your offering.

STEP 9: MINIMIZE RISK

While you may be happy with your sales numbers, have you realized the amounts from your customers? If you are not into cash business, you can never be fully sure about your income till the time you receive the money. Even in cash business, if you were to customize specifically for your client, you may have incurred specific costs in doing so. What happens if your customer does not pay you? So safeguard your revenue from such instances and mitigate revenue risks.

Reflect on all the possibilities to keep your risks at a minimum.

By running through each of the above steps, strategize to build and grow your revenue accordingly. Assuming that you have indeed managed to succeed in all the above steps and achieved your revenue growth, think about your plan to ensure that your revenues are all utilized efficiently.

VARIOUS HUES OF RISK

RISK MANAGEMENT

Even the best businesses make mistakes but are good at correcting, fixing and learning from them, which contributes to their financial growth. A big part of risk management involves managing the probable negative outcomes and creating plans to mitigate the risks. By recognizing the negative factors ahead of time, being proactive and putting the right strategies in place, the business can have a greater chance of success. Risk management is not a one-off exercise. Continuous monitoring and reviewing of risks are crucial.

Risk is a common factor for any business. Be it life or in business, risks are inevitable because taking no risk is the biggest risk. It is important to evaluate your risk and take the right decisions. From a financial perspective, how can you evaluate risks? Remember the word RISK as an acronym.

R: Rewards or returns to be measured and quantified, which will enable you to take the right decision.

I: Investment required in terms of finance, time and team effort must be evaluated.

S: Segregate pros and cons and tangible and intangible benefits so that you are well aware of what lays ahead for your business.

K: Knowingness of the rules, tax implications, facts, market, industry trends, etc., will help you understand the risk. Therefore, do your homework right.

GOOD RISK AND BAD RISK

For a business, there are good risks and bad risks. Every opportunity that creates value can be considered as a good risk. Good risk helps you with your growth plans, creating your strategic vision, etc. Bad risks include non-compliance with laws, ignoring regulations or failing to implement effective policies and procedures.

Successful business owners take good risk and know how to balance risks and rewards. A good risk can bring new markets, new people, new possibilities and so on. Be watchful of your risks and classify them as good and bad risks. What kind of risks are you taking as an entrepreneur?

CALCULATED RISKS

The probability and quantum of a possible loss or damage that your business faces after you have carefully considered all your advantages and disadvantages refer to calculated risks. Risks are inevitable, and it is extremely important to take calculated risks in a business. By taking calculated risks, you become more aware and better prepared for handling the worse possible outcome of a particular business decision.

If you do not take calculated risks, it could result in unexpected or negative outcomes, and it is likely to take you by surprise. So as a shrewd business person, take calculated risks.

FINANCIAL RISK

Financial risk is one of the biggest risks for an entrepreneur as you can run into trouble if the business runs out of finance. Therefore, as an entrepreneur you need to inculcate good financial habits and take the right financial decisions for your business.

Types of financial risks include credit risk, liquidity risk, legal risk, compliance risk, funding risk, interest risk, foreign exchange risk, investment risk, etc.

Few ways to minimize your financial risk are as follows:

- Diversify your income
- Buy insurance

- Limit your borrowings
- Differentiate between good loan and bad loan
- Manage cash efficiently
- Ensure profitability
- Hedge for foreign exchange risk
- Build reserves

RISK MITIGATION

By mitigating your business risks, you tend to lessen the threats posed on your business. So it means taking necessary steps to reduce the negative impact. How can an entrepreneur mitigate risks? It can be done by having a risk mitigation strategy in place and by careful planning and implementation of it.

First, identify the risks, then assess the risk by listing the advantages and disadvantages, calculate the impact of the risk and, lastly, regularly monitor the risks.

If the calculated risks are very high, causing heavy financial damage or impacting brand reputation, it is best to avoid such risks.

While taking risk improves your chances of achieving your future goals, what are you doing to mitigate your risks?

Evaluate right and execute great.

ETHICS AND INTEGRITY

The importance of ethics, integrity and transparency plays a vital role in your business, especially with your customers, as this will go a long way in taking your relationship to the next level and over the long term. Trust and respect are built on the foundation of ethics that you and your team carry and represent. Ethics becomes one of the core values that your organization will be known for. Further, this is also the message you are indirectly giving your team, who are expected to follow suit. Remember that this has to flow from the top for others in the organization to follow suit.

By being transparent with your customer, you are being truthful. For example, if there are hidden/extra costs which will be incurred by the customer, be upfront about it, rather than giving them a rude shock at a later date. This will also enable your customer to plan his budget accordingly. It will build your credibility in business.

Similarly, refrain from using materials of inferior quality just to increase your profits. Such a case may help you win temporarily, but the damage to your name and brand will be permanent. It is better to be known for the quality of your product, which will eventually get you more business—and, thereby, your profits will automatically increase in the long run. Do not opt for shortcuts. They may seem tempting, but having your larger objective in mind will help you with the right decision on the right path. Dell had to pay a fine of over $100 million in 2010, as it misled investors through false accounting to meet Wall Street expectations.

To give another example, if your customer wants the project to be completed by a certain date and you know it is not feasible, be open about it and commit to a realistic time frame, rather than trying to keep the customer happy momentarily.

It is always wiser to under-commit and over-deliver, as that will help you exceed your customers' expectations.

Window dressing, as the name suggests, is used to dress and create an artificial display and does not portray the right picture. It is usually resorted to with the intent to misguide, create a false impression and paint a rosy picture.

At times, financial statements are window-dressed to present a good performance to the shareholders, boost the share price when they are seeking new investment, secure new clients, meet the year-end targets and so on. Financial results are manipulated to project favourable results.

From a legal perspective, window dressing can be considered fraudulent if it is not compliant with the laws and the accounting standards. The well-known examples are Satyam Software and Enron, among others. Extra care and precaution need to be adopted before any sort of window dressing.

A common example of window dressing is when sales personnel inflate the year-end sale to meet their internal target and reverse the sale at the beginning of next year, thereby ensuring that they obtain their sales bonus for the current year. Be watchful of such traps.

As the business owner or business head, you can build the right culture in your organization and lead by example, so as to not get into the culture of window dressing.

INVESTOR RETURNS

One of the prime reasons investors invest in your business is that they seek good returns on their investment. If you do not have an external investor, remember that you are the investor in your business. If your business runs efficiently, there would be good profits. After retaining some amount within the company (depending on the scope for further growth prospects, contingencies of the business and other requirements), the rest can be distributed as returns to your investors, thus giving them a reason to smile.

Here is a pictorial depiction of what will make your investors happy.[1] As the business owner(s), you need to be always watchful of your organization's performance and financial status. Some areas for improving the operating performance of your company are as follows:

- Innovation
- Customer satisfaction
- Excellence

And some areas for improving the financial aspects of your company are as follows:

- Internal controls
- Cost controls
- Efficiency

The abbreviation for both the above are ICE, and so I am referring to them as 'eyes'!

Have an ear for the industry trends in order to be aware of the latest and also perceive any business risks that may be mitigated.

Just as you breathe constantly, you need to be constantly updated with technology developments, adopting effective strategy and lead on expertise. So this forms the nose.

The above leads to increased productivity and increased profits, thereby increasing the returns of your shareholders/investors, thus giving them a reason to smile. When you put these together as a picture, the figure given on next page is what you get.

---

[1] Sumesh, *What the Finance.*

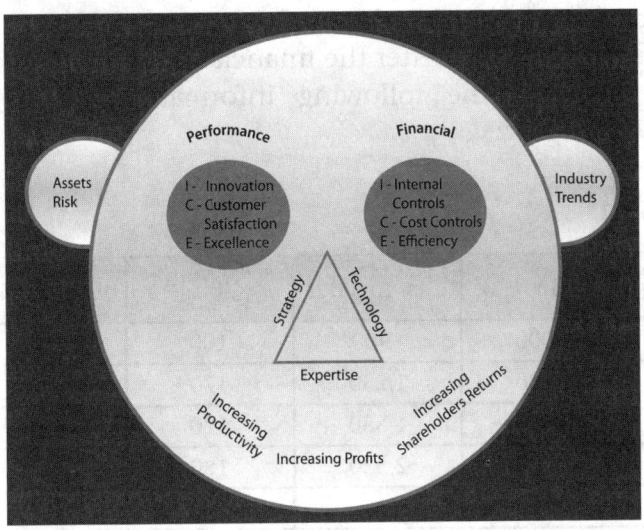

FINANCIAL JAWS

Financial jaws represent the growth of your revenue and margin over a period of time. If you are selling a product at ₹100 each, and the cost of each product is ₹90, it is obvious that you make a margin of ₹10 on each sale. Therefore, by the law of extrapolation, if you sell 1,000 units, your costs will be ₹90,000, and your margin will be at ₹10,000. Here, the profit grows purely by increase in volume.

However, in real life, we know that it seldom happens this way. There may be healthy growth of the revenue but, along with the revenue, your costs are also growing. In such a case, the margins may decrease both as a percentage and also, sometimes, in absolute terms.

When we plot the revenue growth and compare it with the costs, the two lines are meant to represent the jaws. Therefore, in an ideal situation, the wider the jaw, the better the financial performance of your organization. It means that while the revenue increases, the costs decrease and, thereby, the profits maximize. Hence, the wider the jaw, the better the financial status.[2]

Look at the following information for better understanding:

CASE 1

Year	Sales in '000s	Cost in '000s	Profit in '000s	Profit %
1	1,000	900	100	10
2	1,400	1,230	170	12
3	2,000	1,880	120	6
4	2,700	2,520	180	7
5	3,200	3,150	50	2

When the above data is represented as a graph, below is what you get:

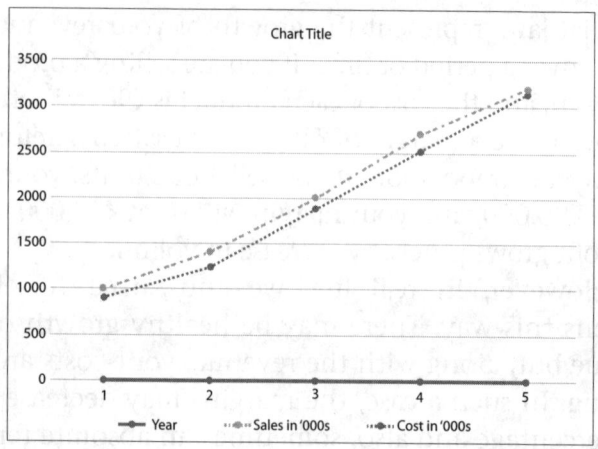

In this case, you will notice that while the revenue has grown year on year, the costs have also grown—

---

[2] Ibid.

thereby, profit has not grown as a percentage of the revenue. In fact, in year 3 and year 5, profits have dropped as absolute numbers as well.

In such situations, ask yourself if you want only the revenue to grow or if you also want the profits to grow and take necessary steps accordingly for the same.

CASE 2

Year	Sales in '000s	Cost in '000s	Profit in '000s	Profit %
1	1,000	900	100	10
2	1,400	1,200	200	14
3	2,000	1,640	360	18
4	2,700	2,250	450	17
5	3,200	2,500	700	22

When the above data is represented as a graph, below is what you get:

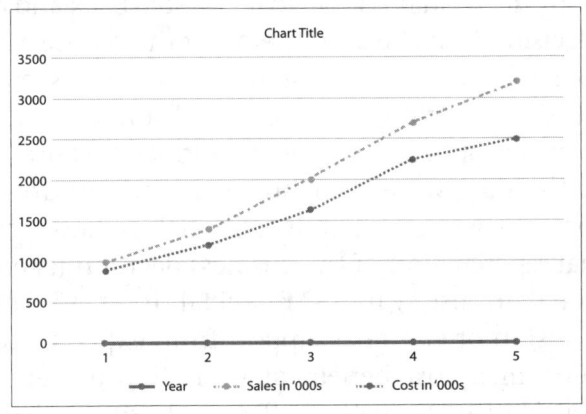

In this scenario, you will observe that as the revenue has grown, the costs have been decreasing, thereby providing a wider jaw, implying that the profits are growing too.

As the business owner, you need to strive to achieve this ideal scenario of increasing revenues and decreasing costs—thereby, the jaws getting wider, indicating maximizing the profits of your business. So you need to focus on widening the financial jaws.

There could be exceptions to the above rule of widening the jaws. For example, you know that you want to achieve a certain target of revenue, as it may be beneficial in the long term for your organization. In cases like these, you take a conscious decision of revenue growth for which you may have to incur higher costs, thereby decreasing your profits but making good the case in future years.

FINANCIAL DECISION-MAKING

As an entrepreneur, you need to make the right decisions so that your business gains financially. While there is no right or wrong in the way to make the decisions, before taking any decision it is good to take a step back and reflect if the decision is in the best interest of the business. Many times I have noticed entrepreneurs as well as business heads taking emotional decisions and not rational ones. Taking an emotional decision is normal because at the end of the day, we are all humans who are driven by emotions. However, what is essential is knowing the financial repercussion of the business decision taken.

You can use various financial tools to validate your decision or else take support from experts. You can also perform a cost–benefit analysis if you seek better financial clarity. Note that all your business decisions need not to be based on cost or the financial impact. What is important in decision-making is what is right for the business and understanding the financial impact for the same. Let me share an example.

A travel start-up was organizing road trips in different parts of the world. At the end of one such regular trip to one of their usual destinations, there was a slight hassle. While returning the 4 × 4 vehicle to the company from whom the travel start-up rented these cars, it was noticed that one of the cars had a slight damage done by a particular customer. However, the customer refused to own it, saying that the damage was already existing when he took the car. There was a lot of drama between the car company, the customer and the tour guide from the start-up trying to resolve who would bear the cost of the damage.

As per the clause with the car rental company, the start-up would not be returned the security deposit in full. The start-up did not want to cough up this amount and neither did the customer. The customer started to threaten that he would damage the reputation of the start-up if he was asked to pay the extra amount. On the other hand, the start-up was concerned that it would hamper the future business relation with the car rental company. And hence the start-up felt stuck and caught in the middle with the customer on the one end and the car rental company on the other.

Ultimately, even though it was not the fault of the start-up, the start-up bore the loss, after understanding the financial implication of bearing the cost. Here is why:

- The start-up as it was still new did not want to lose reputation, did not want the brand image to be scarred and wanted to build goodwill with the customer.

- Similarly, the car rental company was a good vendor to them and did not want to spoil the relationship with them for their future tours.

- Lastly, after doing a cost–benefit analysis, they realized that the start-up had a good profit margin from this trip and therefore paying this amount was still feasible. Even after paying this amount, the start-up was left with a good margin. Hence, the start-up opted to bear the brunt.

The start-up did not stop there. It implemented its learning to mitigate the risk. Hence, for their future trips, it incorporated two steps:

1. The refundable security deposit was to be paid directly by the customer to the car rental agency.

2. Before the start of each trip, a video of the status of the car was shot so that in cases of disputes, it becomes clear who has to bear the cost.

From such experiences and learning, it is key to take measures to plug such loopholes and take careful thought-through decisions. That will ensure the financial success of your business. What else can you learn? I am sharing some business lessons from nature for you to remember while making your business decisions:

Nature	Lesson
Wave	Ups and downs exist in the business; know how to play along with the tide
River	Move along the course and focus on the flow
Lake	Despite the undercurrents, be calm and composed
Mountain	Be strong and mighty to face challenges
Tree	Be grounded despite the winds (of change)
Soil	Be a growth enabler
Forest	Collaborate and thrive
Dune	Shift with changing times
Sun	There exist a new dawn and a brighter side
Moon	Phases of de-growth only to grow again like a business cycle

Nature	Lesson
Stars	Shine on at the right time
Animal	Alertness and agility for sustenance
Flower	Customer happiness and satisfaction
Rain	Gear up for surprises and uncertainties
Rainbow	Be flexible, and unity within the team is the strength

PRINCIPLE OF ESSENTIALISM

During challenging business periods, the times you want to control your expenses and the times when you want to grow your profits, you can resort to the following principle of essentialism.

How does this work? This principle works on classifying your expenses as highly essential, essential and non-essential expenses. While the highly essential and non-essential expenses are fairly straightforward, the grey area is the expenses that fall under the essential category. How can you control these expenses because you are not sure if they are highly essential but at the same time you know that it is not non-essential.

For instance, although the current speed of the internet in your office is not bad, you want to increase the speed of connectivity for the entire organization as it will be faster and ease of working. However, you are not sure if you have the capacity to take on the additional financial burden. You are unsure if this is highly essential or non-essential. So what should you do?

For cases like the above where you are not sure on how to go about, you can choose to fix limits, which can either be a flat sum or percentage of revenue. For example, you can set the limit as the total of the expenses for each month will not be over, say, ₹25 lakh. Alternatively, it can be that the total expenses or the essential expenses will not be beyond, say, 40 per cent of the current month's revenue.

So devise mechanisms which will work effectively for your business. Set them as your guiding principles based on which you can manoeuvre the business. It must be set efficiently that even in your absence, your team knows what needs to be done. Train and guide your team the way you would like them to function so that you can focus on other essential aspects of the business.

LEADERSHIP AND THE ART OF HIGH PERFORMANCE

Be it teams, leaders or organizations, everyone would like to be a high performer in their domain. High performance leads to high profits. By mastering the art of high performance, the team and organization are driven and focused and excel in their work, thereby achieving the desired results. As a business leader:

- Would you want high performance in the work that you do?
- What does it take for you to be a high-performing leader?
- How can you as a leader create and manage your high-performing teams?

An organization is only as successful as its leaders, and the leaders are only as successful as their teams. Thus, by driving high performance in your teams, you can be successful and also contribute to the success of your business. So how can you as a leader drive high performance? If high performance is an art, what would be some of the key ingredients?

Here are some pointers which can enable you and your team to be high performers in the work you do.[3]

---

[3] Sangeeta Shankaran Sumesh, *The Art of High Performance*, 9 October 2020. https://reputationtoday.in/the-art-of-high-performance/

ART OF PURPOSE

Purpose is everything. Knowing why you are doing what you are doing and making your teams aware of it are crucial as a leader. Being purposeful in each activity that you undertake can lead you to high performance. Deep dive and question yourself to get to the real purpose. Know what each action means to you and your team.

ART OF COMMUNICATION

Effective communication plays a vital role in nurturing high performance in the teams. Assumptions, lack of proper understanding and unclear way of expression can come in the way of delivering excellence. Communication should be specific, concise and easily comprehendible by your team.

ART OF INFLUENCING

As a high-performing leader, you must be adept at the art of influencing teams. Leaders can sometimes have an associated ego, which prevents their best to be brought out. Hence, as a leader, you must be mindful of it in order to have a good influence with your teams and guide the team for the best results.

ART OF GETTING THINGS DONE

A successful leader is one who can get things done and deliver accurately and on time. In order to drive excellence within the time frame, you must be capable of getting things done to the best of the team's abilities and drive efficiencies within your team.

ART OF LEADING TEAMS

A leader must know the art of leading the team towards high performance by leveraging on the strengths of each resource. A good leader should not be biased and needs to lead by example. By walking the talk, you must inspire the teams for high performance.

ART OF GROWING

In order to grow further, a leader must step out of the comfort zone. Negative beliefs need to be done away with. Encouragement and positive thinking along with bonding and nurturing the team with high performance culture will pave the way for growth.

High performance is not a destination but a journey by itself. By being better than yesterday and the best version of yourself in whatever work you do, you are on the path of high performance.

Figure 10.2 is the high-performance wheel which you can use on yourself as well as your team members to propel and enable them to be high performers. Get your team member to measure the impact of their high performance. One half of the wheel talks about the impact their high performance can create on themselves and the other half is the impact their high performance can create on the business.

IMPACT ON SELF

Get your team to reflect on the impact on their high performance on the following as these could drive them towards high performance. You can give them a gentle nudge on these to drive high performance:

- *Purpose:* How will high performance contribute to their individual purpose? If the actions are tied up to their goals and interests, it will be easy to relate and thereby drive high performance.
- *Legacy:* What will be the kind of legacy they would want to leave behind even after they move out of the organization? How would they like their successors and colleagues to speak about them and their work done?
- *Emotions:* How would they feel about themselves when they operate at their peak potential and maximize their efficiency? How would it be for them to accomplish tasks consistently and delivering the best?
- *Development:* How would the high performance contribute to their personal success, development and growth?

IMPACT ON THE ORGANIZATION

Make the team understand the positive impact they will create on the organization. Get the team to think about the following:

- *People:* How would the rest of the team and the organization look up at the people who are high performers? What sort of influence will they have on the others in the organization?
- *Customer:* How would the customers feel when high performance is delivered in their service? What sort of impact would that create on the organization?
- *Finance:* Financially, how would the high performance translate for the business? Quantify the financial benefits.

Figure 10.2. Impact Wheel of High Performance

- *Growth:* How will high performance contribute to the long-term growth of the business? What sort of targets can be achieved?

From your past experience with your teams and understanding their individual capabilities, think about the different ways they can perform at the best of their abilities and how you can support their high-performance journey as their leader. Remember that their win is your win, which leads to the business winning.

BUSINESS KARMA

There are times when the situation is not under your control such as lockdown, government rules and regulations, and foreign exchange fluctuations. However, what was, is and will be under your control is the way you are managing your business. Similar to how we have karma or the cause and effect theory in our lives, your business has karma too! Because every action that you have done in your business has resulted in the current status of your business and what you are doing now will be the result for the future of your business. Following are some examples:

- If you have built sufficient cash reserves in the past or managed it well, then the effect will be that you will not have to feel the pressure of cash shortage during the challenging times.
- If your business was solely dependent on one source of supply and the supplier is unable to supply to you, the effect is that your business is impacted.
- Similar story is with the customer. If you have only one major customer, the effect is that your business is in trouble should that customer leave.
- If your collection process was not robust, then the effect is that you have huge amounts due as collections.
- If you didn't hire right and didn't build the right business culture with your team, then the effect is that the team will not stand up for you in times of need.

Take time to reflect on the areas for improvement and learn from them. Think through what the causes are that have landed your business in the current situation, what worked well and what didn't, and get on to rectify them so that in future your business has more good karma.

GAME OF BUSINESS

To make your business performance more interesting for you to track and progress, consider your business as a game. Yes, you read it right—as a game. Gamify the whole process. Rate each step. Set rewards when achievements are made, and if you want you can even penalize when it does not go right or the way you wanted it. The choice is yours. You are the judge and you are the player! So remember to play fair according to the rules that you are setting to ensure that your business is growing to the next level.

Here is a template as a business scorecard, which you can use to create your action plan for your business. You can also brainstorm together with your team to design and create the action plan. The following are simple steps on how you can use the business scorecard.

1. Based on the profit hack wheel for each function, identify the gaps for each subset stated below in the scorecard.
2. If the subset is not applicable to your business, say 'not applicable' and move on.
3. Apart from the stated four subsets, if there are any other specific subsets which you want to include for your business under each function, include it.
4. State the action plan to bridge the gap and related ideas for implementation for your business growth.
5. Set the time frame within which you would like to achieve the action plan.
6. Measure and quantify the impact on the profit by taking the required action.
7. Keep track of the progress.
8. Review periodically. Allot scores.
9. Reward yourself and the team on period progress.

Do what it takes to grow the business. Seek external help if required. If need be, you can consider yourself and your team to work with a business coach to maximize the potential. Alternatively, you can also work with an advisor, consultant or mentor, who can help your business to navigate ahead.

Function	Subset	Gap Areas	Action Plan to Bridge the Gap/ Ideas for Implementation	Time Frame	Quantify Profit Impact
People	R&R Productivity Investment Cost Others				
Customer	Revenue Service Retention Cost Others				
Strategy	Investment Growth Planning Risk Others				
Operations	Investment Metrics Time Efficiencies Others				

(Continued)

(Continued)

Function	Subset	Gap Areas	Action Plan to Bridge the Gap/ Ideas for Implementation	Time Frame	Quantify Profit Impact
Marketing	Top line Cost Threats ROI Others				
Suppliers	Cash flow Legal Cost Management Others				
Technology	Efficiency Threats Risk Cost Others				
Finance	Cost Performance Cash flow Scale Others				

SO WHERE'S THE MOOLAH?

Like you would have realized by now, the moolah or money is there within your business. It is up to you to scrutinize and analyse each aspect of your business to find the money that you want. As an entrepreneur or business head, you have to find these hidden treasures which we have seen across all the chapters of this book. You can make the right decisions and take the right actions towards your business objectives to accentuate your profits as well as have a better cash flow. Do what it takes to achieve your high-performance financial goals.

Some more pointers which can fuel the financial growth of your business are as follows:

- Maximizing the potential of every function of your business
- Thinking and performing with new thought processes by challenging what already exists
- Implementing the action plan which you have designed
- Reviewing progress periodically
- Focusing on your key growth parameters
- Having a person to be your sounding board to bounce off your thoughts
- Working with a Coach as your accountability partner and to challenge you

Look beyond the challenges to start seeing the solutions that you want. Get the right mindset to create the wealth that you want for your business. You can plough the wealth back into your business to enable sustainable and scalable growth, which can be more meaningful for you as well as your business in the long term.

Wishing you and your business the best of high performance and high profits!

ABOUT THE AUTHOR

—

Sangeeta Shankaran Sumesh is 'The Gain Enabler'. A Chief Financial Officer turned Business Coach, enabling high performance and enhancing financial growth for businesses. Her purpose is to serve entrepreneurs, leaders and teams to shine and succeed. She is on a mission to enable, empower and elevate businesses and individuals. She has rich corporate experience of 25 years, including leadership positions with multinationals.

An Independent Director with a listed company and a TEDx Speaker, Sangeeta is a chartered accountant, management accountant and completed executive education from Harvard Business School. She is a credentialed Coach from International Coaching Federation (PCC), and is also a business advisor, professional speaker and the author of the best seller *What the Finance* and *Get High*.

CONNECT - *The Gain Enabler*

www.sss.coach